Teaching Children Joy

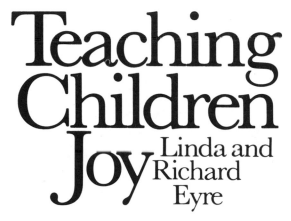

Teaching Children Joy

Linda and Richard Eyre

Photography by the authors

Deseret Book Company
Salt Lake City, Utah
1980

Contents

Introduction   Joy: Who? Why? What? When?
                  Where? How?   1

Section I   SPIRITUAL JOYS   15

    1   Preserving the Joy of Simple Faith
                 and Receptivity to the Spirit   16
    2   Teaching the Joy of Obedience
                 and Decisions   24
    3   Teaching the Joy of Gratitude and of
                 Knowing God as Our Father   36

Section II   PHYSICAL JOYS   45

    4   Preserving the Joy of Spontaneous Delight   46
    5   Teaching the Joy of the Body   58
    6   Teaching the Joy of the Earth   68

Section III   MENTAL JOYS   81

    7   Preserving the Joy of Interest and Curiosity   82
    8   Teaching the Joy of Imagination and
                 Creativity   94
    9   Teaching the Joy of Order, Priorities, and
                 Goal Striving   106

Section IV   EMOTIONAL JOYS   119

    10   Preserving the Joy of Trust and the
           Basic Confidence to Try   120
    11   Teaching the Joy of Family Security,
           Identity, and Pride   132
    12   Teaching the Joy of Individual
           Confidence and Uniqueness   146

Section V   SOCIAL JOYS   159

    13   Preserving the Joy of Realness, Honesty,
           and Candor   160
    14   Teaching the Joy of Communication
           and Relationships   170
    15   Teaching the Joy of Sharing and Service   178

           Index   191

If God's purpose in providing mortal bodies and a physical earth was to increase the joy of His children (and it was), and if the duty and privilege of parents is to assist Heavenly Father in his purposes (and it is), then we should be vitally interested in and concerned with the responsibility of opening the avenues of joy to our children!

Joy: Who? Why? What? When? Where? How?

There are in my memory some small, bright, open places that never close or fade. I remember as if it were yesterday the moment when the doctor put our just-delivered, still-wet, first child on my trembling arm.

I remember the outside things: the antiseptic hospital smell, the unique combination of joy and fatigue on my wife's face, the exquisite perfection of each tiny new finger and toe. Even more, I remember the inside feelings: the sighing relief, the welling joy, the almost irresistible urge to throw open the hospital window right then (at 3 A.M.) and announce the new arrival to the world.

Slid in, just under the joy, was another feeling: the weight of responsibility, the sudden remarkable reality that this soul, this spirit, this tiny real person was ours now, ours to raise, her destiny so totally trusted in our inexperienced, untried, untrained parenthood.

Within the next hour there were calls to new grandparents and the fun of hearing their voices jump from grogginess to excitement. Then, finally, with new baby and new mother fast asleep, there was nothing more for me to do but drive home. By then it was early-summer dawn, with deserted streets and delicate, pale gold sky. Spontaneously, as I drove, I started to pray out loud. Somehow the joy, the marvel, the miracle of birth had lifted my spirit higher, closer, so that it seemed natural right at that moment to just talk to God. "Thank you" was the essence of the prayer; thank you for something so great I could not comprehend, for something I could not imagine I was worthy to receive.

After the thank you, all that was left was the desire (not the obligation) to repay, to commit, to promise—to somehow make my thanks more than just words by pledging that I would honor the stewardship, that I would strive to be a *great* father. Suddenly the fullness of the word struck: "Father." The Father of us all had just allowed me to take that role, that title (his role, his title) for one of his children. I remember the exact words that came next in my prayer: "Oh, Father, help me to be a father."

There is another open space in my memory, two and a half years later. We were flying home after a visit to Grandma's. Little Saren had her face pressed close to the rounded pane as we took off.

"Daddy, look at the tiny people! They're like the ants."

"What ants, honey?"

"The ants on the ant hill—see—hurrying back and forth."

"What ant hill, honey?"

"You know, by the groundhog holes."

Then I remembered: last spring, eight months before, walking through a field showing her ants and groundhogs. She still remembered; the impression was still there!

Children start as a blank slate for us to write on, and they retain everything we write. Absorbing, learning from every experience, every exposure, they are unexposed film, and pictures are registering as fast as the shutter can click.

Amazed at Saren's memory, I reflected on the previous eight months. During that time she had learned to talk, to recognize the seasons, to relate to a baby sister, to ask questions . . . a thousand things. I remember thinking, "I hold the chalk; I can write whatever I will on this fresh slate, and though it may be partially erased later, the underlying traces will always remain." What had I written on her slate so far? What had I taught? All I could think of were incidental things, questions she had asked or thoughts that came, unplanned, to my mind. And love. Of course I had taught her love. (Or is that what she had taught me?)

In that moment, as I marveled at my daughter's amazing receptivity, I asked myself: *Is love enough?* What else should she learn? What can I give her, teach her, show her? The thoughts of stewardship flooded back. Was I doing all that I could? Was I keeping that early-morning pledge to be a great father?

By the time our plane landed, I had decided to spend the five remaining days of my vacation reevaluating my fathership. The next morning I went to a bookstore and bought eleven "raising children" books. I read everything from Montessori to Dreikurs, from Dobson to Suzuki. The books didn't agree on very much (different people with different ideas), but what they did agree on made me feel worse rather than better. They agreed that most of a person's intelligence, character, and outlook on life are formed by the time he is five years old, that a small child's mind is an intricate computer, with every circuit open, ready to be programmed.

When I finished my reading, the basic question was still unanswered: What is the most important thing children should learn during this most important learning time? The books covered so much, and were collectively so complex. The authors left me with an impression of good people who had tried hard, who had studied the wisdom of other people and of their own minds, but who somehow lacked the one beam of pure light, the one clear, hard, diamond-gem answer to what life is really for, what little children need to gain in order to find their own lives, their own dreams, and later, their own Maker. The next day I went back to the office, the vacation over, the question unresolved.

A few months later Saren turned three and wanted to go to nursery school. We looked at several and found none

we liked. They each fit one of two categories: either
academic, pressure-to-learn, first-grade-for-three-year-olds,
or do-nothing, baby-sitting, day care. The first seemed determined not to let children be children. The second
seemed undetermined to help children do anything. We
knew neither was right for Saren; we doubted either was
right for any three-year-old. Somehow it was easier to see
that they were wrong than to see *what* was wrong, or what
they lacked that Saren needed. We looked more and
reached out further—Montessori schools, experimental
schools, then specialized schools: dance, art, music. It was
clearer to us than ever before that the incredible, open-
circuit mind of a three-year-old needed stimulation in
massive doses. The question was what form that stimulation should take. We realized that we now knew rather
precisely what the question was and what the answer
wasn't. I sat down and wrote out the question: "What is
the most important thing (other than love) to give and to
teach preschool-age children?"

Then I made a list of some of the wrong answers: to
read and write a year or two early, to do basic ballet steps,
to know the names of the birds and animals, to add and
subtract and multiply and divide.

The next specific moment I remember was just a few
weeks later. We were driving up a winding canyon road . . .
bright autumn day, early morning . . . children both asleep
in the back of the station wagon. The beauty of the day
somehow created an atmosphere of free thinking, and the
two of us talked randomly. Ideas came easily; so did questions.

What were we looking for that we didn't find in the
preschools? What would we teach if *we* had a preschool? If
we could give our children one gift, what would it be?

Suddenly the questions started knitting together. The
last answer came first—we would not give possessions, not
wealth, not even education. We would give happiness—

joy—the gift that everyone wants for himself, and that everyone wants to give to those he truly loves.

Once the word *joy* came into the formula, everything else began to fit. Children teach us so many kinds of joy: spontaneity, living in the present, being totally interested and so often thrilled with life. But they must learn other joys: sharing, service, conscious goal achievement, searching and finding, planting and harvesting.

Can young children gain these varieties of joy? Can they actually experience them at a tender age? Yes! All true forms of joy are simple and pure. Children can feel them more easily, more naturally than adults.

The answer, then, to the question *Is love enough?* is "No!" And the answer to *What else?* is "Joy!"

If children, in their most impressionable years, can gain the capacities to experience and recognize real joy—if joy flows into the clay of their lives before it hardens—then perhaps they may *inherit* joy as a lifetime gift.

Our thoughts continued to tumble together that autumn morning as we wound down the canyon. Things fit together quickly, as they often do when a breakthrough, long sought, is finally reached. Out of the thought-tumble came two personal commitments: (1) to start a "joy school," to teach what we hadn't found in other preschools, and (2) to write this book, to say what we hadn't found in other books.

The first objective was a joy to accomplish. We bought a house and converted it (a wall torn out here, a sandpile put in there) into a nursery school. We formulated and classified our ideas as we repainted walls. We defined and dissected and analyzed the concept of joy as we landscaped the yard. We worked out joy-teaching, joy-experiencing methods as we brought in toys and play equipment.

By the time the school opened we had developed a curriculum of fifteen separate "joys," and we had found many other parents who shared our view that the word *joy* summarized what we most wanted our children to gain.

Among our fifteen joys were five that children are born with, forms of joy that we hoped the school would buttress and encourage, strengthen and preserve. The other ten were joys we felt children had to *gain*, capacities they did not inherently possess but that they could feel if given the opportunity.

The fifteen joys now become the chapters of this book. The school and the home have been our laboratories.

If children, in their most impressionable years, can gain the capacities to experience and recognize real joy (if joy flows into the clay of their lives before it hardens), then perhaps they may inherit joy as a lifetime gift.

Back to that autumn morning when we first began to think about teaching children joy. We first determined—

—that joy is the basic purpose of life,

—that a person's capacity for joy is formed mostly in his first five years of life,

—that our greatest stewardship (parenthood) is best fulfilled by giving children joy,

—that joy can be effectively sought and taught,

—that joy can be divided into a number of specific and particular types of joy,

—that the sources of these individual joys can be discovered and developed,

—that the gospel of Jesus Christ is the key text of these joys,

—that, in its basic form, each joy is simple enough to be grasped and understood by small children,

—that we (the two of us) wanted to make the teaching of joy to our children our highest priority,

—that to crystallize and specify our thinking on teaching joy to children, we would write a manuscript.

Once we had decided all of this, we still faced the formidable task of "subdividing" joy, of defining the word, pinpointing its sources, breaking into its various forms. We had in mind many different feelings and experiences and situations that generated various levels of joy.

What we needed was a filter, a collator, some sort of framework to press all the random joys through that would organize them into neat stacks so that we could talk about them by category, so that we could dissect each stack and see what each was made of, and so that we could feed those basic ingredients into the formative minds of our children.

We had to organize and categorize joy. The question was not "Which joys can we teach children?" We had already decided that children are capable of experiencing the basic levels of all joys. The question was "What is the full range of joys that man can experience, and how can we teach the capacity for each to little children?"

Finally, we held three fireside chats with groups of people whose minds we respected. Without telling them why, we asked each person to recall some specific moment of joy, some particular time and place in his life when he was consciously aware of deep, genuine happiness. We paused for fifteen minutes, asking each person to pin down a particular moment. Then we tape-recorded their answers. Thirty people on each of three separate nights gave us ninety individual responses; none were duplications. Then we tried to organize and catalog the responses. What was the essence of each? Where were the similarities?

We shuffled and rearranged, and finally, one morning we found ourselves with five groupings of joy, each with three subgroups. Each of our ninety "instances of joy" fit nicely into one of the fifteen categories. The result was a table of contents for this book. Take a moment and look at it. Notice that there are three spiritual "joys," three physical "joys," three mental "joys," three emotional "joys," and three social "joys."

Our effort to categorize the joys led us to one intriguing and unexpected insight into children and their capacity to learn joy. In each of the five categories of joy, children are born with the basic seed of joy that, if nurtured properly and kept alive, can become the tree on which the two related joys can grow and develop.

In each of the five areas, then, there is one joy to *preserve* and two to *teach*. For example, the mental joy of curiosity and interest, which children are born with, can, if it is encouraged and preserved, become the basic capacity or vehicle for learning the joy of imagination and creativity and the joy of priorities and goal achievement. As a second example, in the social joys, if we can preserve a child's natural openness and candor, that *inherent* joy can become the cup into which we pour the *learned* joys of communication and relationships and of sharing and service.

It is as though the Lord sent each small child down with fifteen precious gems. Five were finely cut, highly polished; ten were rough, uncut, but potentially valuable. Parents are the jewelers. This book is a manual for keeping the five polished stones bright and for cutting and finishing the ten rough ones. Each chapter—each joy—is presented in six simple parts:

1. *Examples and description.* To clearly identify and isolate what the joy is, one "child example" and one "adult example" begin each chapter. In the "joys to preserve" chapters, the child example comes first, since we learn the joy from them. In each of the "joys to teach" chapters, the adult example comes first, followed by a child example that demonstrates that small children can experience that particular joy.

2. *Methods.* Several methods are then suggested, each with the objective of helping the child to experience and identify the particular joy. These are not presented in exhaustive detail, but rather in simplified, abbreviated, outline form so that the parent can catch their essence and then apply them with his own special personality and interpretation. Virtually all of the methods listed can be used both individually in the home by parents and in group situations (Mothers' groups or Joy Schools). Methods particularly suited to groups are noted in the text by an asterisk (*).

3. *Family focal point.* Most parents, with the daily

concerns of occupation and obligation, cannot make up lesson plans or think consistently about multiple methods. They can, however, remember and implement one "family focal point" for each joy. Each focal point is a simple family idea (a clear habit or tradition or practice) that keeps that joy prominent and conscious in the minds of family members.

4. *A story for children,* one that illustrates and dramatizes the joy.

5. *A reading list* of children's stories that are about "that joy." While there may be scores of children's books that could apply to each chapter, this is a very selective, hand-picked list of the ones we personally consider to be the best.

6. *A postscript* of real-life results—examples of children's increased capacities for joy. These were reported by teachers at the Joy School, or by parents of children attending the school, or have been taken from our own experience.

The fastest summary and justification for the notion of *Teaching Children Joy* comes through a quick overview of the six questions: who, why, what, when, where, and how.

Who?

Little children, our greatest stewardship, who come to the earth "holy and incapable of sin."

Our brothers and sisters, who come to us as children in our charge.

Our children, who are the future of this world and of God's kingdom.

Why?

Because rearing children is the greatest single obligation of earth life.

Because rearing children is the greatest single opportunity of earth life.

Because "No other success can compensate for failure in the home" (David O. McKay); because "The most important work you will ever do will be within the walls of your own home" (Harold B. Lee); and because "Home is the place to save society" (Spencer W. Kimball).

Because Christ said, "Feed my lambs." Many people qualify as lambs, but none so obviously and profoundly as our own children.

Because the Lord commands us to! "Bring up your children in light and trust." (D&C 93:40.) "Teach [them] to pray, and to walk uprightly before the Lord." (D&C 68:28.) "Train up a child in the way he should go; and when he is old, he will not depart from it." (Proverbs 22:6.)

What?

First, the basic physical necessities of life: food, clothing, shelter.

Second, love—so unconditional and so deep that it can never be doubted.

Third, joy, which is the goal of life (2 Nephi 2:25), recognized by all men of all ages as the most priceless gift, a product of understanding and living the Savior's teachings (John 15:11), and a framework for all the specific things we want to give our children. (Confidence, calmness, testimony, security—each is a kind of joy.)

When?

In their preschool years, when 80 percent of a lifetime's learning takes place and 50 percent of one's basic intelligence is gained.

In their preschool years, when basic personality, character, ability to relate and cope, capacities, emotional structure, outlooks, and attitudes toward others are formed.

In their preschool years, when we have them before schools, social activities, and friends begin to gradually and systematically take a percentage of their time away from our sphere of influence.

In their preschool years, when they are blank slates— when we can write on those slates what we will without having to erase what is already there. (The older they are, the harder it becomes to erase.)

Where?

First of all, in the home and family, where the emotions and relationships can exist that teach the child the most important and basic joys.

Second, in a group with other children, where social and creative joys can be most easily taught and where peer relationships and confidence can be formed.

It is interesting to hear the frequently repeated debate on preschools:

"Preschool children should be with their families, with their mothers."

"But they need exposure and social relations with other children."

"They can get that with neighborhood friends and in Primary."

"But to get ready for school, they need structured group situations."

"Mothers cannot pass off the teaching responsibility to others."

"No, but some kinds of things can only be taught in groups."

Both sides of the argument are right, and the two sides are not necessarily opposed to each other. It is true that the responsibility is the parents', that children need the parental input, that the bond formed by a parent teaching and showing a child is valuable, irreplaceable. But it is also true that some things (indeed, some joys) can only be taught in groups.

The "bring-together" answer is *mothers' groups.* Mothers agree to a teamwork situation that gives children the beneficial experience of being in a friend's home and being taught a particular "joy" by a friend's mother. Mothers (a dozen or so) alternate the responsibility. Two or three times a week the group meets at one of the homes. This book is the manual, the method-giver. Each mother comes up for her turn only every three to six weeks.

Joy Schools (patented name for schools operated or franchised by R.M. Eyre & Associates, Inc.), where they are organized, accomplish the same thing. Children are allowed to attend no more than three short, half-day periods per week, dramatizing the fact that the schools are supplements rather than substitutes for parents.

How?

By creating situations in which children actually sample or feel a certain joy. Children learn by reinforcement, and nothing reinforces better than joy. Therefore, if a parent can get a child to actually feel and recognize a particular joy, then he has given the child the capacity to repeat that joy by doing once again the thing that caused it.

By showing joy yourself. Children will emulate what they see in you. The beautiful by-product of teaching children joy is that, in order to do so, you must experience more joy yourself.

By role-playing and utilizing other forms of imagination that place children in situations that are "as if" they were experiencing a particular joy.

Through identifiable stories where children vicariously feel the joy.

Through "reinforcement-recall": remembering and thinking back (thus reliving) to a moment when one of the joys was felt, remembering not only the moment, the incident, but also the actual *feeling*.

By systematically concentrating on one of the fifteen joys each week. Parents should read the chapter on each week's joy at the beginning of that week. They should then plan together just how and when to teach it. Thus, once every few months, each joy is taught for a full week.

By sitting down once a month as parents and evaluating together the progress of each child on each joy, pinpointing the particular joys that need the most work.

By simply being aware enough of the various joys that you can convey and teach them to your children subconsciously.

Shortly after we started the Joy School, and as we were beginning this book, Linda made an entry in our collective diary that presents an overview of the theory of this book. She called her thoughts "I.Q. vs. J.Q."

"We started our school because of our strong disagreement with the common supposition that the greatest thing that a child can possess (or that we as parents can help him to attain in order for him to 'succeed' in today's society) is a high I.Q. Too much stress is placed on young children's abilities, on being able to put together numbers and letters quickly, on manipulation skills. The world at large seems to be overly aware of 'How soon will my child read?' or 'Just listen to him count or recite.' While these things do have their place, we strongly believe that real happiness, contentment, and ability to cope with the world lie in a child's J.Q. (joy quotient). Ponder, for a moment, the quality of a child's life once he has obtained confidence in his own ability to make decisions, to enjoy and be aware of nature, to understand another person's ill feelings, to set a goal and accomplish it, to share with and serve his friends, and to see himself as a totally unique individual with a great deal to offer to others. Each of these are joys that can be taught, and we are of the opinion that the ideal time to teach them is before the age of five and before the beginning of formal education. With a foundation of these 'joy' concepts, the other abilities often associated with I.Q. will come quickly and naturally. By teaching a child joy, we can give him both a calm spirit and an active mind."

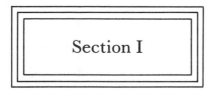

Section I

SPIRITUAL JOYS

Small children, with their pure faith and fresh innocence, can quickly grasp and feel joys of the spirit. Spiritual joys intensify other joys. For example, we recognize that the world is beautiful, but it seems even more beautiful when we realize that our Father made it for us.

Gratitude *is very nearly synonymous with joy. Spiritual joys teach us of the Being to whom our gratitude must be directed. He has told us: "I have no greater joy than to hear that my children walk in truth." (3 John 1:4.) "They shall also teach their children to pray, and to walk uprightly." (D&C 68:28.)*

"If [parents] have one child or one hundred children, if they conduct themselves towards them as they should, binding them to the Lord by their faith and prayers, I care not where those children go, they are bound up to their parents by an everlasting tie, and no power of earth or hell can separate them from their parents in eternity." (Brigham Young.)

"I know that if ye are brought up in the way ye should go ye will not depart from it." (2 Nephi 4:5.)

Preserving the Joy of Simple Faith and Receptivity to the Spirit

1

□ *"Pray in your families unto the Father." (3 Nephi 18:21.)*

"Parents, have you ever noticed that your little children have exercised faith for you when you have been sick? The little daughter, seeing you sick, will lift her heart with a pure, angelic-like prayer to heaven; and disease is rebuked when that kind of faith is exercised. God bless the children!" (Discourses of Brigham Young, *p. 206.*)

I. Examples and Description

A. *Child:* The most painful illness I remember ever having was a severe ear infection. I was five years old. I have clear recall of that day: the warm, hollow tock, tock of the pendulum clock, the brow-furrowed look on my mother's face, and my father's simple, clear explanation of the priesthood's power to heal the sick. I suppose, at that age, there was little inclination *not* to believe . . . this was simply the way God had told us to use his power to cure sickness. "Let's do it," I said. "I want to be well."

I remember the dizzy warmth of heavy hands on my head. I don't recall the words of the blessing but I do recall, right after it, walking back into my room and waiting, wondering if it would be five minutes or five hours until I was better (never thinking to wonder *if* it would work).

Children are believers. For a child, prior to the world's infection of criticism and pseudosophisticated doubt, it is easy and natural to believe in God, in a loving, father-like God who is real, who cares, who hears and answers the prayers of his children.

Children are acutely receptive to feelings, to atmosphere. Put a child in a calm, happy place and you can almost see him absorb the peacefulness and joy. Anyone who can develop this childlike faith (or repossess it) can be lifted and touched by the Holy Spirit. Parley P. Pratt tried to describe what that Spirit can do: "The gift of the Holy Ghost adapts itself to all these organs or attributes. It quickens all the intellectual faculties, increases, enlarges, expands, and purifies all the natural passions and affections, and adapts them, by the gift of wisdom, to their lawful use. It inspires, develops, cultivates, and matures all the fine-toned sympathies, joys, tastes, kindred feelings, and affections of our nature. It inspires virtue, kindness, goodness, tenderness, gentleness, and charity. It develops beauty of person, form, and features. It tends to health, vigor, animation, and social feeling. It invigorates all the faculties of the physical and intellectual man. It strengthens and gives tone to the nerves. In short, it is, as it were, marrow to the bones, joy to the heart, light to the eyes, music to the ears, and life to the whole being." (*Key to the Science of Theology,* Deseret Book, 1978, p. 61.)

Who would not want to feel this great spirit? Isn't it interesting that the description "fits" most children so well?

Not long ago, riding alone with six-year-old Saren, I asked, "How is school going, Saren?"

"Fine." (Ask a not-much-thought question, get a not-much-thought answer.)

I tried again, harder: "Saren, how do you usually *feel* inside while you're in school?"

"I have a good, calm feeling inside, Dad . . . [pause] because I know my family loves me and I know Heavenly Father loves me [pause] so it makes me feel warm and like *I* love everybody."

B. *Adult:* Can people keep that feeling? that spirit? that childlike trust? I think of my Grandma Swenson because she had childlike faith. I first realized that when I was ten and she was seventy. She was at our house, and my father called on her to lead our family prayer. She literally cried unto the Lord. (She always cried when she prayed.) She asked as if she knew he heard. I remember thinking that she sounded like my little brother when she prayed. I remember that she talked to God as though he were a father and she were a child. I remember that her prayers were always answered.

Again the question: Can we learn more from children than we can teach them? Somewhere there is an eternal law that relates humility, teachability, and childlike faith with receptiveness to the Holy Ghost.

II. Methods

A. *Strive to keep the Spirit always in the home.*

What a joy can be found in the spirit of a home! In a world so high-strung, so selfish, so untrusting, what a strength it is to step out of the world and into the home— like stepping out of war into peace, out of hard tension into soft serenity, out of the wind into the calm and stillness of the eye of the storm.

How can we make it that way? We can do it through—

—Prayer: personal, open, to a loving Father; family prayer.

—Kindness and sensitivity, to people and things.

—Service to each other.

—No quarrels in the home—go outside if voices must be raised.

B. *Help children explore and compare.*

There is a profound connection between childlike joy and childlike faith. How can we as parents preserve the faith and "belief tendency"? How can we bolster it and encourage it enough that it can weather the criticism and cynicism of the world? Perhaps the way lies in doing the opposite of what may come naturally.

The first impulse is to protect and isolate—to build a wall between the child and the doubts and falsehoods of the world. Actually, the danger of cynicism, like the danger of atheism, is greatest not among those who are exposed and who carefully explore, but among those who don't. The best way to help a child prepare his basic faith is to help him explore, to encourage questioning and testing, and to let him see our total confidence in the ultimate answers of the gospel.

In the long run, encouraging children to question and explore will not only strengthen their testimonies, but it will also develop their knowledge, broaden their tolerance and respect for other beliefs, and open the doors of their minds to new ideas.

C. *Protect the calmness of the home.*

Remember Ozzie and Harriet, the television show? Not

very dramatic or exciting—but I used to love to watch it as a child. Thinking back, I believe it was because of the calm feeling it always gave me. There were no catastrophes; when someone made a mistake, Ozzie would say, "Well now, that's too bad, isn't it—here, let's fix it so it won't happen again."

Children, when their physical wants are filled, are inherently calm and peaceful; only as we teach them frustration and agitation do they change.

D. *Bring spiritual influences into the home.*

If you have the priesthood in your home, use it often in your family. We have a tradition of giving each child a father's blessing on each birthday.

Some say the priesthood should be used only in time of real need. But is there not real need when a father is leaving on a three-day business trip? when a five-year-old is worried about starting school? when a new pregnancy begins? when a little boy can't sleep because his tummy aches? One great purpose of the priesthood is to bless the home and family. The Lord is displeased not by excess use, but by lack of use.

Also, talk about the Holy Ghost. Comment on the moments when his presence is felt; ask the children, "How did you feel during that blessing?"

E. *Have early-morning "quiet time" and family devotionals.*

The spirit that begins a day so often stretches through and fills the whole of that day. If a day can get off to a peaceful, spiritual start, children will have an inner peace that will buffer them against aggravation and worry even several hours later.

Begin breakfast at a set time each morning. Teach children that the time before breakfast is "quiet time," when we get dressed and think peacefully about our blessings and about the day ahead. Everyone whispers. There are some squeezes of hands and pats on the head and smiles of love and pride in each other.

Breakfast starts with a simple "devotional." A one-verse scripture is read. (Often a parent can read it a line at a time and a child can repeat it.) The idea or message of the scripture is discussed in simple terms, and then the morning kneeling prayer is held.

Properly applied (it takes a little time for small children to feel the peace of the idea), this procedure can turn the first hour of a family's day from a time of noise and confusion to a time of peace and order.

III. Family Focal Point: Family Prayer

Family prayer, in one form or another, is held in most genuinely religious homes. But there are two factors that can make the practice particularly meaningful to children:

A. *Regularity.* Families ought to have two specific times set aside every day for family prayer. At least one dependable, committed time, when every member is there, is essential. For most families, just before breakfast and just before dinner are the most reliable times. If necessary, get up early to assemble for prayer. Let children see that it is the highest priority.

B. *Thoughtfulness.* If family prayer becomes too routine, too automatic and habitual, children will begin to view it as ritualistic rather than relevant. Take two or three minutes together before starting the prayer to discuss what you as a family are particularly thankful for that day. Discuss what needs the family has and what should be asked for. Then ask someone to say the prayer.

IV. Story: "How Heavenly Father Helped Me"

Every other chapter in this book has a particular story. This opening chapter does not, because personal stories have the greatest effect in preserving and developing a child's faith.

Each parent should accept the challenge of thinking of a clear, simple incident from his own life that illustrates the power of faith or the working of the Spirit. When a child hears his parent say, "This is a story about how Heavenly Father helped *me*," he will listen, he will remember.

V. Reading List

Baird, Coleen. *Seven Days and Prayer.* Salt Lake City: Deseret Book, 1980.

Barnes, Kathleen H., and Pearce, Virginia H. *Testimony.* Salt Lake City: Deseret Book, 1974.

_____. *What Is a Miracle?* Salt Lake City: Deseret Book, 1975.

Bickerstaff, George. *The Gift of Prayer.* Salt Lake City: Bookcraft, 1976.

_____. *My Special Family.* Salt Lake City: Bookcraft, 1977.

Hays, W., and Hook, F. *My Jesus Book.* Cincinnati: Standard Publishing Co., 1964.

_____. *My Thank You Book.* Cincinnati: Standard Publishing Co., 1968.

VI. Postscript

A. Little Saren, five, had gone with her father, who had a speaking engagement in a ward some thirty miles away. The meeting had been very special and the spirit seemed very strong, partly because of the twenty-three nonmember investigators attending that day with missionaries. On the way home, Daddy asked Saren how she liked the meeting. She said, "Well, I didn't understand the words too well, but it really felt good in there. It felt real soft, just like in family home evening."

B. One day, a week or so after a long family talk on thinking before we pray, the children were called in from their play in the year's first snow. Mother was called on to offer the evening family prayer. It was a fairly normal prayer, but when it was over, four-year-old Josh looked seriously at her and said, "Hey, you forgot to say thanks for the snow. If you would think a little harder you'd remember these things!"

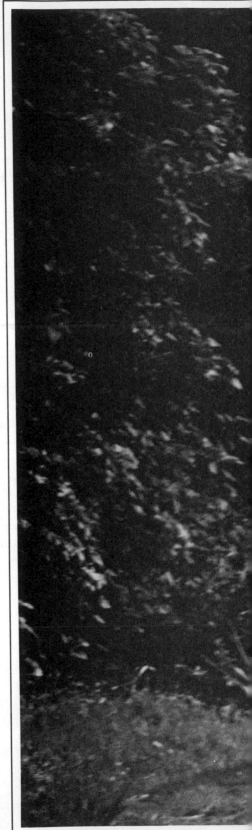

Teaching the Joy of Obedience and Decisions 2

☐ *"The home is the best place in which to develop obedience which nature and society will later demand."* (*David O. McKay*, Stepping Stones to an Abundant Life, *Deseret Book, 1971, p. 289.*)

"Train up a child in the way he should go: and when he is old, he will not depart from it." (*Proverbs 22:6.*)

I. Examples and Description

Wrong decisions avoided and right decisions made produce happiness. Many of life's decisions are made simply by the existence of law: moral law, natural law, governmental law, God's law. Obeying a law always yields a reward; breaking one inevitably produces punishment. One who knows and is committed to a law makes *in advance* decisions related to that law. (Most of us have decided in advance not to jump off tall buildings because we know and respect the law of gravity.) To those who know and accept other laws, it can be equally natural to decide in advance to marry in the temple, to finish one's education, to turn the other cheek, to stop and help those in need, to attend church and fill church assignments, to go on a mission, or to live the Word of Wisdom.

The other decisions, the laws without a right and wrong, the laws with many alternatives, are somewhat more difficult; yet they constitute one important aspect of why we are here on earth: to learn to weigh, to analyze, to think, to ponder—to make free choices with our free agency. The Lord stands ready, as he states in Doctrine and Covenants, section 9, to confirm and assure us in our decisions if they are right, and to give us a "stupor of thought" (to tell us to start over) if they are wrong.

The joy of obedience and of correct decisions is the joy of progress, of being on the right course. Some might say that this "course-keeping" joy is the prerequisite to eternal joy.

A. *Adult:* I have a good friend who likes to talk about decisions. He says: "The Lord has made so many of our decisions for us. He's told us what to do, but he's left us with the excitement of deciding how and when and where and with whom. For example," he goes on, "I feel sorry for anyone who tries to decide what to do with one-tenth of his earnings, or where to get married, or what to do on Monday nights. The Lord has already told us these things. I save my mind for the hard decisions, for the ones where the teacher hasn't already given out the answer sheet."

This friend relishes decisions. He loves to lay out the alternatives, to think things through, to decide—and then to take his decision to the Lord for confirmation. I see two consistent joys in him: the joy of obedience (in the things God has already decided), and the joy of decisions (in the things he has left up to us).

I asked my friend once just where he learned to think that way. He said, "As a child in family councils and in private interviews with my father."

B. *Child:* Romping out of the candy store, our four-year-old Saren, just learning to count money, discovered she had been given change for fifty cents rather than a quarter. Initial excitement: "I've got more money than when I came, *and* the candy." Then conscience: "I'd better give it back to the man." Then the real joy as she came back out of the store: "Daddy, he said he wishes everyone was honest like me!" There is true joy in simple, voluntary obedience.

That story reminds me of another time, another store, another child—Saren's father. I was age eight, and buying my first bicycle. I had twenty-five dollars, saved up from Grandma's gifts and from collecting and returning coat hangers and pop bottles. There were two used bikes in town for twenty-five dollars, one a red Schwinn and one a silver Silverchief. I couldn't choose. First I wanted one, then the other. My wise father took me back out to the car, found a large white sheet of paper, and drew a line down the center. "Let's list the reasons for the red bike in one column and the reasons for the silver bike in the other," he said. I did. I remember the thrill of thinking in a way I had never thought before. When the list was done, the silver bike was selected. (After all, no one else had one like it.) I

kept that bike for ten years, and the memory of the joy of
deciding on it never dimmed.

There is tremendous joy and satisfaction in learning
that things are governed by laws. Psychologists tell us that
small children usually believe that their desires control circumstances and cause things to happen. The time when a
three- or four-year-old realizes that this is not the case, that
things happen independently of his wants, can be a very
traumatic time. Or, if he is being taught about laws in a
positive, constructive way, it can be a time of real awaken-
ing joy.

In the gospel it is not only interesting but eternally
instructive that the first law taught, the first covenant
entered, is that of obedience. Laws and discipline are out-
growths of love—of God's love. Too many of us adults
think of laws as restrictions, confinements; it's too bad the
words *commandment* and *law* sound so repressive. We should
remember that the Ten Commandments could also be
called "The Ten Ways to Be Happy." Obedience to law
actually gives freedom by rescuing us from the natural
consequences and confinements of broken laws. Freedom
and truth are first cousins.

The priesthood is the power to control laws. Faith is the
belief in laws we can't understand. Children, even small
ones, can grasp these truths—sometimes more easily than
adults can. Children need to be given the latitude to make
their own decisions. They will make some wrong ones, but
will learn, with our help, from the consequences. While
they are young, the decisions and their consequences will
not be weighty enough to do permanent damage. And by
the time decisions become important, they will know how
to make them.

II. Methods

A. *Teach children to differentiate between situations governed
by law and situations governed by decision.*

*1. The picture game: Show various pictures and ask with each one, "Is there a law, or do we decide?"

    a. car going past speed limit sign (law of the land)

    b. person walking by a cliff (law of gravity)

    c. child getting dressed (we decide which shirt)

    d. children fighting (law of God)

    e. child buying ice cream at 31-flavor store (we decide)

*2. Make up stories that get to points of "What should he do?" (Is there a law that tells him, or does he make a decision?)

3. Tell a story about a home without any rules. What happens? Is the family happy? (The story could also be about a school without rules.)

B. *Expect and demand "perfect obedience."*

Teach children that "perfect obedience" means to say, "Yes, Mommy," or "Yes, Daddy," and to obey immediately whenever they are told to do or not to do something. This may seem rather arbitrary or militaristic, but children inherently love discipline—it gives them a type of security that is otherwise unavailable. Always say "please" to children so that they feel your respect and love. Make "please" a trigger word by teaching them that whenever they hear it, they should say, "Yes, Mommy" and obey. When they do not respond quickly, just say the words "perfect obedience" to remind them to say "Yes, Mommy."

Children should know that they have the right to ask why, but that perfect obedience (with the "Yes, Mommy") is expected right after the why answer is given.

C. *Design frequent opportunities for decision making.*

1. Have two kinds or colors of juice to choose from.

2. Let the children draw pictures, choosing only three colors to use.

---

*Asterisks indicate methods that are best used in group situations.

*3. Let the children choose only one tool to work with in sculpting clay or whipped soap flakes.

4. Let the children choose the bedtime story.

*5. Set up a treasure hunt where a series of correct decisions leads to a surprise or treasure.

6. Let the children choose what clothes to wear. Help them think it through: "Is it warm?" "Will I get dirty today?"

7. Let the children choose what to spend their nickel or dime on—or whether to save it.

8. Make family decisions in family council. (What should we do at our next family home evening? What should we do this Saturday?)

D. *Tell stories about wise or foolish decisions you have made and what the consequences were.*

E. *Reinforce and discuss the consequences of decisions.* "What will happen if you do that?" "Will that make your sister happy or sad?"

F. *Discipline.* Parents must make their own decisions about the methods of discipline, but certain principles always apply.

1. Children should be disciplined in private rather than in public.

2. Children will repeat the activities that attract the greatest attention. The key, therefore, is to make a bigger thing of the attention given (encouragement and reinforcement) for doing something *right* than of the attention given (punishment) for doing something *wrong*. Give lavish, open praise for the right, and quiet, automatic discipline for the wrong.

3. Children should know the reasons for the laws they are expected to keep and should think of obedience in terms of observing laws, not in terms of obeying people.

4. Children find great security in consistent, predictable discipline.

5. Discipline should be thought of as a way of teaching truth.

6. Punishments should be administered only when laws are broken. When children make wrong decisions in areas not governed by law, their punishment should come through the natural consequences of those wrong choices. (If a child forgets his coat, he gets cold and needs no other punishment.)

G. *Teach the principle of repentance.* Children should learn that through genuine repentance they can avoid punishment. Teach children the beauty of repenting toward each other. We have learned in our family that when one child teases another, or hurts another in some way, a simple form of repentance can restore good feelings much faster than punishment. We remind the guilty child, "You'd better repent." Repentance, for one of our children, consists of four things: (1) a hug for the other child; (b) a request, "Will you forgive me?"; (3) a statement, "I'll try not to ever do that again"; and (4) asking Heavenly Father for forgiveness that night in prayer.

III. Family Focal Point: The Family Laws Chart

One of the most memorable family home evenings we have ever had was the night we agreed to the "family laws." We had prepared a framed piece of heavy posterboard and put a nail in the wall to hang it on, and now we explained to Saren (four) and Shawni (three) that this was to be a list of our family laws.

We talked for a moment about "nature laws" and "country laws" and "church laws" and, as usual, got the best definition of the word from Saren.

"What is a law then, Saren?"

"Something that, if you keep it, you're happier, and if you don't keep it, a bad thing happens to you." The stage was now set.

"What are some laws for our family that, if we keep them, will make us happier?" The list gained momentum. Saren's openers got Shawni thinking and the list grew:

"Don't hit other little girls."

"Don't plug in plugs."

"Don't ruin things that are not for ruining."

"Say the magic words (please, thank you, excuse me)."

We had to help with some that they didn't think of:

"Stay in bed when put there."

"Sit down in back seat when riding in a car."

"Don't walk while holding the baby."

"Don't go in the road unless holding Mommy's or Daddy's hand."

"Mind with no backtalk." (Saren added a clarification here: "But we *can* ask why!")

We really didn't realize, at the time, what a help the list would be. Rather quickly the children grasped the idea that they were obeying laws that *they* had helped decide on, laws that would make our family happier.

Some time later, in another family home evening, we decided as a family which punishments should go with which laws. The children decided that a little spank was the most appropriate punishment for hitting and for certain other serious or dangerous violations. They decided that "going to our room" should be the penalty for whining and for certain of the other laws. On some laws, we decided that one warning should be given before a punishment would be required. By the raise of hands, we sustained each punishment and wrote it on the "family laws board."

IV. Story: "Cheekey and the Laws"

Cheekey was a baby monkey. He lived with his sister and his mother and father in a tree. Their tree was in the jungle. In the jungle there were some laws. They were called the Jungle Laws. Do you know what laws are? (Things that you must do right or else you get punishment.)

Do you know what a punishment is? (Something sad that happens when you break a law.)

There were two laws in Cheekey's jungle. One was that

whenever you were in a tree, you had to hold on with your hand, or your foot, or your tail. What do you think the punishment was if you broke that law? (You would fall!)

The other jungle law was that if you saw a lion coming, you had to quickly climb up a tree. What do you think the punishment was if you broke that law? (You would get eaten up!)

In Cheekey's own family tree, there were two family laws. One law was that you couldn't go out of the tree without asking. Why do you think they had that law? (So Cheekey wouldn't get lost.)

Why didn't his mother and father want him to get lost? (Because they loved him.)

What do you think the punishment was if Cheekey went out of his tree without asking? (His mother gave him a little swat with her tail right on his bottom.)

Why did his mother do that? (So he wouldn't go out of the tree again.)

Why didn't she want him to do it again? (Because she loved him and didn't want him to get lost.)

The other monkey family law was to never drop your banana peels on limbs of the family tree. Why do you think they had that law? (So no one would slip on them and fall out of the tree.)

Why did the monkey family decide to have a law like that? (Because they loved each other and didn't want anyone in their family to get hurt.)

What do you think the punishment was for breaking that law? (A little swat on the bottom.)

Why would the mother do that? (Because she loved Cheekey and wanted him to remember not to do it again.)

Now, I'm going to tell you the things that happened to Cheekey one day. Sometimes there were laws to tell him what to do and sometimes there weren't any laws and he could decide for himself.

When Cheekey first woke up in the morning, he had to stretch and yawn, and he almost let go of the branch. Was there a law to tell him what to do? (Yes—hold on or he would fall.)

Then he looked at his two hats, a red one and a green one. Was there a law to tell him which to wear? (No, he could choose whichever one he wanted. He chose the red one.)

Then he wanted to climb down out of the tree to find a banana for breakfast. Was there a law to tell him what to do? (Yes—ask his mother so she would know where he was and he wouldn't get lost.)

He found a big banana and a little banana. Was there a law to tell him which one to choose? (No—he could choose either one he wished.) Cheekey chose the big one because he was very hungry.

While he was walking back to his tree, he saw a lion. Was there a law to tell him what to do? (Yes—climb up a tree quickly or the lion would eat him!)

Cheekey climbed up a tree. After the lion went away he went back to his own tree and wondered which limb to sit on to eat the banana. Was there a law to tell him where to sit? (No—he could choose any limb he wanted.)

When he peeled the banana, was there a law about the peel? (Yes—don't leave it on a limb.)

Cheekey had a fun, safe day. It's fun and safe when you know the laws and do what they say and it's fun to decide things when there isn't a law about them.

V. Reading List

Arnold, A. *The Yes and No Book.* Chicago: Reilly & Lee Books, 1970.

Coombs, P. *Lisa and the Grompet.* New York: Lothrop, Lee & Shepard, 1970.

Gunthrop, K. *Curious Maggie.* New York: Doubleday and Co., 1968.

Johnston, J. *Edie Changes Her Mind.* New York: G. P. Putnam's Sons, 1964.

Leaf, M. *Fair Play.* New York: J. P. Lippincott Co., 1939.

Lowrey, J. S. *The Pokey Little Puppy.* New York: Golden Press, 1942.

Odor, R. *Cissy, the Pup.* Chicago: Child's World, 1977.

Rice, I. *A Long Long Time.* New York: Lothrop, Lee & Shepard, 1964.

Waber, B. *Ira Sleeps Over.* Boston: Houghton Mifflin Co., 1972.

Williams, B. *If He's My Brother.* New York: Harvey House Publishers, 1976.

VI. *Postscript*

As the teacher was reading a story, Travis kept bothering Andy, who was interested in the story and was trying to listen. After twice reminding Travis that it was "listening time," the teacher removed him from the group and Andy was heard to say, "I'm glad we have rules in this school."

Jamie's mother told this experience: As they pulled up to a large office building that Jamie's father had recently built, Jamie said, "Daddy, that was really a big decision you had to make on where to build this building, wasn't it?" Then her younger sister added, "Was it a good decision, Daddy? Did it make you happy?"

Teaching the Joy of Gratitude and of Knowing God as Our Father

3

☐ *"And in nothing doth man offend God, or against none is his wrath kindled, save those who confess not his hand in all things, and obey not his commandments."* (D&C 59:21.)

"For we labor diligently . . . to persuade our children . . . to believe in Christ." (2 Nephi 25:23.)

"I love these little people, and it is not a slight thing when they who are so fresh from God love us." (Charles Dickens.)

I. Examples and Description

A. *Adult:* I remember a powerful speech I once heard fifteen years ago, but it seems like last week. For half an hour, the speaker discussed how infinite and incredible the universe is and how insignificantly small we are. He said man has discovered 7×10^{15} stars. Then he asked, "If each star were represented by one page in a book, how thick would the book be?" Five feet? A hundred yards? Ten miles? No—as thick as the distance around the world six hundred times!

Each of us, he said, is a speck on one tiny earth that revolves around one of those 7×10^{15} stars. We were awed; we felt so small that we wondered if we were even still there. Then he made this point: "When I look out on the night sky, I see the handiwork of God, but when I look upon your faces, I see God's offspring."

What I remember most is the warm glow that settled on that meeting—the secure, privileged joy that struck my heart as I contemplated the fact that I was more important to my Father than all of his stars, that they were made for me, that I was his son.

Can children feel this joy? Of course they can! It is based on simple, childlike faith—faith that God not only lives, but also loves us as his children.

As we come to think of God as a loving, personal Father, we begin to feel a natural expansion of gratitude. One reason God told us to be like little children is that children feel gratitude so easily and naturally, and God knows how closely related gratitude is with joy.

If we can understand that God's definition of a joyful man is "a grateful child," then we may begin to see one of his most quoted phrases—"Be like a little child"—as the method of achieving one of his other most-quoted phrases: "Men are that they might have joy."

B. *Child:* How well I remember the day when our fifth child, Jonah, was born two months premature. That evening, with him in an incubator and breathing with a respirator, with Linda under sedation at the hospital, and with my own mind full of worry and fear, I returned home and explained to six-year-old Saren, five-year-old Shawni, and three-year-old Josh about the baby's need for our prayers. We knelt down together by the bed. Josh prayed first: "Bless my new little brother Jonah that he will breathe better and get big so he can play with me." Then Shawni: "Heavenly Father, I love you. Thank you for Jonah. Help him stay here on the earth with us because we love him." Then Saren: "Our dear Heavenly Father, we love you. Thank you for sending little Jonah down to be in our family. Help him to breathe by himself. Help him to come home soon to his new family so we can hold him and love him." As I held those three children to me, the world was blurred by my tears, but the faith in my heart had never been more clear. Their prayers, by the way, were answered.

Children teach us so much. I remember asking Saren one day, as we drove home from the grocery store, what she was grateful for. She felt gratitude for things I hadn't even noticed: the warm heater in the car, the snow on the pine trees, the frozen peas we had just bought, the stove we had to cook them on, our fingers so we could hold hands, for we were holding hands right then.

One day I bought eighteen-month-old Jonah his first balloon. He was awe-struck, overcome with excitement as he batted it, squeezed it, sat on it, squeaked it. He toddled over to me again and again to show me, always beaming with delight, and that night he leaned his little head on my

shoulder in a special way that I knew meant "thank you."
Little children can feel such genuine joy. If we can teach
them that God gave them all things, then all things can
give them joy.

II. Methods

A. *Prayer.* Discuss before family prayer: What are we
grateful for? What does Jesus look like? How can Heavenly
Father hear our prayers? How does he want us to talk to
him? What are the things we really need that we should
ask him for? Children who think of a Heavenly Father and
Brother can pray with the realness and candor that the
Lord has told all his children to use. We can pray often
together and help children to understand that they can
pray always in their hearts.

B. *"Favorite Things Wall."* The wall or board discussed
in chapter 6 can be a great prompter of gratitude and of
recognizing the small things for which we feel thankful.

C. *The "Aren't We Blessed" game.* Have a tradition of
saying, whenever there is a special moment of pleasure or
gratitude, "Aren't we blessed!" Say it as you sit down to a
meal; when you get home safely after a long drive; at the
high point of a family home evening; after opening presents at Christmas; as you see someone less fortunate. Just
say, "Aren't we blessed!" Be sure the children understand
the meaning, and they will soon be saying it too—at just
the right moments.

D. *Role-play the premortal existence.* All children are there
with Heavenly Father and can see a mother and father
down on the earth. Heavenly Father sends down one at a
time—oldest first. He stays up there watching us, hoping
we do the right things and have happy families, listening
carefully to our prayers and answering them. Then the
father or mother gets old, goes back up, and tells Heavenly
Father what a happy life and happy family he or she has
had.

E. *Fasting.* Even small children are capable of missing
one meal and of feeling the special temporal gratitude that

comes from fasting. Put some money on the table and dramatize that "these four dollars will be saved by not buying one meal today, and we'll give these four dollars to poor people who miss many meals." Sometimes the sponsorship of a particular child through an overseas "help fund" makes this more dramatic. Have a picture of the child; explain that he only gets one meal a day, that "our four dollars buy food and clothes for him."

F. *Turn other joy forms to spiritual ones.* All of the appreciation methods in chapters 5 and 6 (joy of body, earth) can turn to spiritual forms of gratitude as the element of thanks-oriented prayer is added.

G. *"Gratitude input."* Tell a child how blessed he is. Do it often, pointing out specific blessings: you have two great sisters, you are strong, you can run fast, you have two grandpas, you have a kitten, you have a healthy body, you have a smart brain.

H. *"Gratitude poster."* At Sunday dinner, decide on one particular thing to be grateful for during the coming week. (Start during the first weeks with simple things like rain, food, schools, clothes. Later include more complex things like freedom and self-respect.) Have a child "draw" the item for gratitude each week on a sheet of paper and put it on the wall by the dinner table where it is noticed and talked about often and mentioned in prayers. Each week as the previous poster comes down, save it with the others to bind together at the end of the year as the "gratitude book."

I. *Answer out loud a child's prayer.* Do this just once in a while to give him the idea that God is real and really does hear prayers. For example: Child says, "Thank you for the beautiful flowers." Parent says, "You're welcome. I made them because I love you, and I'm glad you like them." Explain that you are just showing what God might be thinking while he listens to the prayer.

III. Family Focal Point: The Family Testimony Meeting

In the mission field we had a practice as companions of

bearing our testimonies to each other each Sunday morning. It always surprised me that, even though we'd been together all week, feelings and insights came out in those private testimonies that were never mentioned otherwise. The spirit and atmosphere of the occasion made it a time of true openness. All barriers were down, and we said what we felt.

We do the same thing now as a family each fast Sunday before our dinner. If it was helpful and beautiful in the mission field, it is even more so now in our family. Each person takes a turn right around the table, even the little ones. (The very little ones get some help, just as they would in a prayer.) Each family member expresses his gratitude, his feelings, his testimony. It is a time when children learn to stand up and express themselves, when little differences get apologized for and cleared away, when gratitude is truly felt and expressed, both to each other and to God, and when testimonies are voiced, nourished, and given room to grow.

As children are old enough, they are encouraged to say only what they really feel, and to never say something just because it is expected or just because someone else said it. It is a sharing time, a time to share gratitude, conviction, perspective, and love.

IV. Story: "Your Story"

This is a story about you. Before you came to live with us, you lived with Heavenly Father. Heavenly Father was called God. He had a great many children, and he loved them all very much. You had a different kind of body then. It was made out of spirit, and you couldn't learn quite as much or feel quite as much with that kind of body. You wanted a body like Heavenly Father's, one made out of flesh and bones. The way to get that kind of body was to be born on earth. Heavenly Father had made the earth for us so that we could learn many things. You knew that things would be kind of hard on the earth and that you would have some sad days. But you really wanted to come here because you knew the earth was so beautiful, and you wanted to get a body and have a mother and a father and brothers and sisters.

You and Heavenly Father looked down and tried to find just the right family for you. When you saw your mother and father you said, "That's the family I want." Heavenly Father agreed, so he started a little body for you inside your mother's tummy. At first it was just a tiny little seed, but it grew and grew, and when it was big enough for you to be born, Heavenly Father put your spirit into that little body.

Before he did, he asked you to do two things while you were down on the earth: first, to love him and to love all his other children in the world; second, to help your family and someday to have a nice family of your own.

Heavenly Father knew that you would be a baby for a while after you were born and that you would forget a lot about him and about what he told you, so he gave us some special books that would help us remember where we were before we were born, and what he told us. He also picks out certain special men on the earth that he talks to so that they can tell us what he wants us to know.

More than anything else, Heavenly Father wants us to come back and live with him after we die. If we love everyone and have good families as he told us to, then we can go back and live with him in heaven.

V. Reading List

Baird, Coleen. *Seven Days and Prayer*. Salt Lake City: Deseret Book, 1980.

Barnes, Kathleen and Pearce, Virginia H. *Forever and Ever*. Salt Lake City: Deseret Book, 1975.

Bickerstaff, George. *Before I Was Born*. Salt Lake City: Bookcraft, 1974.

—————. *My Body Is a Temple*. Salt Lake City: Bookcraft, 1978.

Field, R. *Prayer for a Child.* New York: Collier Books, 1941.

Griffin, Glen C. and Mary Ella. *About You . . . and Other Important People.* Salt Lake City: Deseret Book, 1979.

Hays, W., and Hook, F. *My Thank You Book.* Cincinnati: Standard Publishing Co., 1968.

Johnston, D. *Stop, Look, and Listen.* Cincinnati: Standard Publishing Co., 1977.

Larson, D. *I Am a Child of God.* Salt Lake City: Bookcraft, 1971.

—————. *My Gift from Jesus.* Salt Lake City: Bookcraft, 1972.

Pearson, Carol Lynn. *My Turn on Earth.* Hollywood, California: Embryo Music Co., 1977. (Also available in record form.)

VI. *Postscript*

A. Five-year-old Shawni had been allowed to hold her new baby brother for a moment. She sat on the couch and gazed at his little face for several moments, lost in her thoughts. Then in a caring, sweet little voice she said, "You tiny little one, I bet you're thinking about heaven where you were a few days ago. You haven't forgotten how Heavenly Father looks yet, have you?"

B. Josh, age four and a half, finished one of his first "by myself" bedtime prayers. As he jumped into bed his mind was still on the prayer. He said, "Dad, it's really neat that Heavenly Father still loves us even though we've been gone for a long time, and he's got really really good ears too, doesn't he? Because he can hear us from way up there when we pray."

In his prayer he had said he was thankful for water. As I tucked him in, I asked why. He said, "Because without water we couldn't flush the toilet . . . and there would be no goldfish . . . and no popsicles."

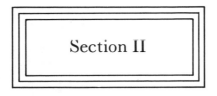

Section II

PHYSICAL JOYS

"The morning stars sang together, and all the sons of God shouted for joy" at the prospect of a physical existence. (See Job 38:7.)

Preserving the Joy of Spontaneous Delight

4

☐ *Do you want to know the purpose of mortality? Then listen to the sound of a child's laughter.*

I. Examples and Description

A. *Child:* I was upstairs in my bedroom; eighteen-month-old Josh was right below me downstairs in his sister's room. At first I thought he was crying, but as I listened again, I heard it for what it was: a loud, spontaneous belly laugh. I knew he was down there by himself, because I could hear his sisters with Linda in the kitchen, so I sneaked quietly down to observe. I peeked through the door just in time for the next peal of laughter. Josh, his back to me, sitting on his haunches, was facing Saren's bed. The bedspread, hanging to the floor, suddenly bulged and then lifted to reveal Barney, our big black Labrador, squirming out from under the bed. There was something funny about Barney's shifty-eyed, kind-of-sheepish look as he pushed his head out from under the spread. Josh laughed so hard he fell sideways. Then he promptly crawled under the end of the bed, Barney following, crawled back out from under the bedspread, and turned to watch Barney come out again.

Josh's laugh made me smile, made me feel free. Adult laughs are too often sarcastic or boisterous or somehow forced and brittle. Josh's spontaneous laugh pealed out like a thousand bells—the kind of free, delighted laugh that most little children have and most adults lose.

There is often a paradox in adult minds. On one hand, we admire spontaneity; we speak of the free spirit, the unconventional, with at least a lingering trickle of envy. On the other hand, we associate maturity with words like *sophistication, reserve,* and *proper.* Too often parents convey the inhibitions of "the other hand" to their children. How many times have you seen a parent give a sideward, brow-furrowed look of scorn to a child whose spontaneous delight and enthusiasm was "socially improper." We let our own inferiorities and inhibitions stamp out the spontaneity in our children, and we let our schools and institutions do the same thing. If we are not careful, it becomes harder to preserve and protect in our children the joys they were born with than to teach them the ones they came here to learn.

B. *Adult:* I was alone one day, walking to lunch on a busy Boston street. Ahead was an old man, begging, "Any spare change?" The young businessman ahead of me brushed him off. "No, no—sorry." Too busy. Life is a pattern, each man with an image of himself. The businessman was sophisticated, on a time schedule: "can't be interrupted," "don't stop for this unsavory character," "he's not on my daily calendar." Then I came up to the beggar. I saw his face. I saw character mixed with tragedy in the old eyes. "Come on—come to lunch with me." Spontaneous, spur of the moment. The man was surprised. I was surprised. I'll forget other lunches, but never that one. The incredible story of a broken man's break—it did him good to tell it; it did me good to hear it. He left with a full stomach and with a flicker of hope because someone had cared and listened. I left happy because I had helped, but also because I had done something spontaneous—free—open.

II. Methods

As with each of the "joys to preserve," the key method is encouragement and reinforcement. Children will repeat what they are praised for.

There are many ways to encourage and sanction a particular behavior; perhaps the best way of all is by participating in that particular behavior yourself. (And perhaps the great benefit of preserving the natural, childlike joys in children is that we may recapture them in ourselves.)

A. *Get excited with children.* Swallow your sophistication—be a child with them, emote with them. When they say, "Oh look," you say, "Wow, yes." Don't say, "Calm down, son," or "Not here, dear." Let them be your teachers. They are the experts in spontaneity—do what they do. Live in the present with them. Praise them for watching, and watch with them what they watch!

B. *Help them relive spontaneous joy moments by remembering.* "Remember when we saw the bird pulling up the worm, Josh? Wasn't that great?" "Remember at the picnic when the grasshopper jumped into the potato salad? Didn't we laugh hard?"

C. *Do spontaneous things with them.* "Hey, Shawni, instead of a bedtime story tonight, let's put on your pajamas and go to the ice cream shop for a cone before you go to bed." "Josh, your mom looks tired. Let's put *her* to bed for a nap, and you and I will fix dinner."

D. *Make spontaneity a high priority.* Place enough value on spontaneity that you let it happen even if it's a little inconvenient. Suppose you are walking outside on a warm summer afternoon and you spot your two-year-old stomping with delight in his first puddle. Resist the urge to yank him out with a "No, no!" Take off his shoes and let him do it. (Or take off *your* shoes and do it with him!)

E. *Surprise-oriented group games.* Play games together in which the adults share and encourage the children's spontaneous delight, such as hide-and-seek and musical chairs.

F. *Opening packages.* Wrap things up—share the surprise as children open them. Have them guess what's inside before opening.

G. *Put new surprises into old fairy tales.* It's amazing the delight that the mixing of two familiar fairy tales can cause. "While the three bears were walking in the woods, they heard a funny little man singing a song. 'They'll never guess that Rumpelstiltskin is my name.'"

H. *Do things with children that are a little silly and that show how acceptable it is to enjoy unexpected things.* (1) Put a mitten on the doorknob and "shake hands" with the door. (2) Pop popcorn in a popcorn popper without a lid (put the popper in the center of a large sheet so the popped kernels fly up and fall down on the sheet). (3) Get up and do a little dance when the music and the mood hit you. (4) Catch grasshoppers in a field (in a delighted way).

*I. *Engage in the kind of play that produces exciting and unpredictable results.* (1) Blow bubbles with a straw (in a glass of soapy water, or in the tub at bath time). (2) Finger paint with thick paint. Let the children mix colors. Let them try it with their feet. (3) Play in the water with empty plastic bottles, straws, or funnels.

III. Family Focal Point: The Family Treasure Chest

We have a "treasure chest." It is just an old wooden box, painted many beautiful colors, with a big combination lock on it. The children know from experience that there is always a surprise in it.

Once or twice a week, on special occasions or perhaps for rewards, it is opened by Daddy, the only one who knows the lock's combination. It is amazing how delighted a child can be with one small piece of candy, or a pinecone, or even a small sponge so he can help wipe off the table. Anything, so long as it comes out of the treasure chest, produces spontaneous delight.

IV. Story: "The Bears Save the Baby"

(This story is for children familiar with the stories of "The Three Bears" and "Rumpelstiltskin.")

Once upon a time there were three bears; a daddy bear, a mama bear, and a little baby bear. One day they were having soup for dinner and the baby bear said, in his wee, little voice, "This soup is too hot." "It is," said the daddy bear in his deep, big voice. "Let's go for a walk in the woods while it cools off."

So they did.

They skipped off into the woods singing their favorite

song, which was "The Bear Went Over the Mountain."
When the song ended and their voices were quiet, the baby
bear said, "Shhh, listen—I hear someone else singing."
They all listened, and they heard a little song coming out
of the deepest part of the woods. "Let's go see who it is,"
said the mama bear. They crept very quietly, as only bears
can do. Pretty soon they were close enough to hear the
singer clearly. His was a strange, croaky little voice, and
the song went like this:

> "Today I cook, tomorrow I bake
> The next day the queen's child I take.
> For she will never, never proclaim
> That Rumpelstiltskin is my name."

The bears got close enough to see through the trees and
into a little clearing. They saw a tiny, wicked-looking man
dancing around his fire. He sang the last line again, "For
Rumpelstiltskin is my name."

In a tiny whisper, the daddy bear said, "Come this
way," and the three bears walked quickly and quietly away
until they could not hear the little man anymore. Then the
daddy bear said in his deep, big voice, "Who was that?"

"He was bad," said the baby bear in his high, squeaky
voice.

"What was he singing about?" asked the mama bear in
her soft, gentle voice.

Daddy: "About the little princess, I think."

Baby: "He is going to take her away from the queen."

Mama: "Unless the queen can guess his name."

Baby: "She'll never guess a funny name like Rumpelstiltskin."

Daddy: "Unless we tell her."

Baby: "Let's run to the palace."

Off went the three bears as fast as their legs would carry
them. At last they saw the palace. At first the guard was
afraid when he saw them, but the mama bear said in her

soft, gentle voice, "Don't worry, we have come to tell the queen the name of the bad little elf."

"You know his name?" said the guard. "We've all been trying to figure it out. Come with me right this way."

When they found the queen, she was crying and sobbing. "How can I ever learn his name?"

"We know it, we know it," said the baby bear in his high, squeaky voice.

"What? Who are you?" asked the queen, looking up.

"We found the little man in the woods," said the big daddy bear respectfully. "He didn't see us but we heard him say his name."

The queen clapped her hands with joy, and the baby bear whispered in her ear, "Rumpelstiltskin."

That night when the little elf showed up, laughing and thinking that he would take the baby, the bears were carefully hidden under the table so they could watch.

"Well, you don't know my name," he said, "so I'll be taking the little princess."

"Let me guess first," said the queen. "You said I had three guesses."

"All right, but hurry," said the elf. "You can never guess it."

The queen was enjoying herself now. She decided to use all of her guesses before getting it right. "Is it Joshua?" she asked.

"No, no, no," laughed the little man, rubbing his hands together. "Guess again."

"Is it Jonah?" said the queen.

"No, no, no, no. You'll never guess."

"Well," said the queen, "for my last guess, is it Rumpelstiltskin?"

The elf turned red in the face with anger. He stomped his feet so hard that he disappeared right through the floor and was never seen again.

There was a great celebration at the palace, and the

queen invited the bears to stay and to become special palace guards. The bears thanked her but said they had to get back to their house to see if their soup was cooled off yet.

V. Reading List

Aliki. *Is It Blue as a Butterfly?* New York: Prentice Hall, 1965.

Asheron, S. *The Surprise in the Storybook.* New York: Grosset & Dunlap, 1963.

Barret, J. *Animals Should Definitely Not Wear Clothing.* New York: Atheneum, 1970.

Baun, A., and Baun, J. *Know What? No, What?* New York: Parents Magazine Press, 1964.

DeReginiers, B. *What Can You Do with a Shoe?* New York: Harper & Brothers, 1955.

Lund, D. H. *Did You Ever.* New York: Parents Magazine Press, 1965.

Slobodkin, E. *Caps for Sale.* New York: William R. Scott, 1947.

Stone, J. *The Monster at the End of the Book.* Racine, Wisc.: Western Publishing Co., 1971.

Zolotow, C. *Not a Little Monkey.* New York: Lothrop, Lee & Shepard, 1957.

VI. Postscript

Lisa (age 4): "I'm going to stay with my grandma tonight—all right?"

Teacher: "Do you like to do that?"

Lisa: "Yes, and Grandma likes it too. She says she likes me to come 'cause I make her laugh a lot."

Teacher: "Oh? How do you make her laugh?"

Lisa: "She's funny. Whenever I laugh, she laughs."

Teacher: "And what makes you laugh?"

Lisa: "I don't know. I guess it's just the 'happy' coming out. And do you know what?"

Teacher: "No, what?"

Lisa: "Grandma's pretty old, but I can do something better than she can."

Teacher: "Oh? What's that?"

Lisa: "Laugh."

Then Lisa laughed.

Teaching the Joy of the Body 5

□ *The body is an instrument for feeling. We feel things with our bodies that would otherwise be unknown to us. The beauty and challenge of life are that we choose what our bodies will feel. I want to choose joy.*

I. Examples and Description

A. *Adult:* It wasn't that he was extraordinarily healthy, it was just that he enjoyed things about his physical body that most take for granted. He was a farmer, middle-aged, living in the flat, middle plain of America. He loved the hard, sweat-producing work in his field. "The hot sun limbers up my body," he would say, "makes me feel more loose and easy." He liked winter work as well. "My lungs like to feel that cold mornin' air a-fillin' 'em, and if I work hard enough, in ten minutes, I'm warm as summer."

On Wednesday evenings, after a long day's work, he played softball. He was the oldest member of the team. He said that part of the enjoyment was the competition and the company, but most of it was the physical joy. The catch, the throw, the hit—each, for him, was a momentary splurge of physical pleasures, a bump of joy.

The same physical joy showed in a different way when he took out his old fiddle. His tone was sometimes wrong—his position always was—but the rhythm in the twitch of shoulder and tap of toe told me that his wide smile reflected uninhibited joy.

This man loved his senses and his senses loved the earth. He'd close his eyes so he could listen better to whippoorwills. He'd stop just to breathe the lilac breeze in early May. He'd let the soft black soil sift through his fist just to feel its texture. And when his wife baked apple pie, he would hold the first bite in his mouth for half a minute "to be sure I taste it all."

He found amazement and wonder in the natural processes of his body—the rejuvenation of sleep, the fuel of food. Much of this world's progress and possessions had passed by this man, but his ability to feel the joy of his own body twinkled his eye and brightened his face so that the world looked back with envy.

B. *Child:* Here is a conversation I had with my three-year-old.

"Why did Heavenly Father give you a body?"

"To skip with!"

"To skip with?"

"Yes."

"I see. What's the best part of your body?"

"The eyes."

"Why?"

" 'Cause I see the flowers."

"Oh?"

"But the nose is too, 'cause I smell them."

"Do you hear them?"

"No, but if you close your eyes you do hear teensy little things."

"Like what?"

"Wind and trees."

"How do they sound?"

"Swish, swish, but quieter than that."

"Any other parts of the body you like?"

"The tongue to talk—you hold onto it and you can't talk—try it—say my name."

"Unghun—uwam."

"See!" (Laughter)

"Shawni, does your body make you happy?"

"My body *is* the happy!"

The spontaneous delight and built-in curiosity of little children make them receptive to the joy of the body. They are perfect pupils, but they still need teachers. The sensing equipment is built in—they receive the sensation—but they need to interpret it to feel its joy. A child's senses are more acute than ours, but the joy of the body lies in understanding what we sense, and that is where the teaching comes in.

What joy is in the body! The joy of work and of hard

purposeful effort, the joy of singing, the joy of sport and activity, the joy of tenderness and physical touch, the joy of controlling physical matter. Children have a tendency toward them all. Softly feel a baby's head, rough-house with a two-year-old, watch a three-year-old squeeze shapes from a square block of clay, and you'll see the opening melodies of the body's joy.

Inhibition and fear take away the body's joy. Children learn inhibitions and fear from us. How can we avoid it? First, we must help them to try physical things, without intimidation, embarrassment, or fear. We must help them begin to sense the simple enjoyment of the functioning of their bodies. Then, beyond that, we must help them find and concentrate on the particular physical things that they do especially well, the things in which they are gifted, be they sports, music, crafts, dance, or whatever their own particular gifts suggest.

II. Methods

A. *Learning the names of body parts.*

*1. Play "Simon Says." The leader gives various commands: "Touch your tummy." "Lift your left foot." "Close your eyes." The rest of the players follow a command only if it is preceded by "Simon Says."

*2. Play "Hoky Poky." Players stand in a circle and act out this rhyme: "You put your left foot in, you put your left foot out, you put your left foot in and you shake it all about. You do the Hoky Poky and you turn yourself about. That's what it's all about—hey!" Rhyme is repeated with each part of body.

*3. Make a large puzzle of the body out of heavy cardboard pieces for children to put together. As they do, they name each part and tell what it can do.

B. *Teaching appreciation for the body.*

*1. Focus the children's attention on one sense: Close your eyes (or use blindfold). Ask: "What can we hear?

Listen closer—is there anything else we can hear?" (Do this outside and inside, in city and in country.)

Close your eyes and ears. What can we smell?

Close your eyes and ears. Taste something and identify it.

Close your eyes and ears. Feel something with your feet and identify it.

2. Pretend you don't have certain body parts, then try to do things. For example, pretend you have no fingers— just fists—and try to put on your shoes.

With no eyes (blindfolded), try to put a piece in a puzzle. With no thumbs (tape them to fingers), try to pick up a penny. With only one hand (other one in pocket), try to catch a big ball. Without bending knees (keep legs straight), try to walk up stairs.

*3. "What is it?" game. Blindfold the children. Then let them hear and smell and touch and taste various things and try to identify them. Use things with interesting textures (sandpaper, cotton, polished stones); different sounds (bottled water, marbles in a box, a bell); distinct odors (perfume, popcorn, pickles); distinct tastes (sugar, salt, peanut butter, root beer).

*4. Identify sounds. Tape-record a variety of sounds; play them and have children identify what they are.

*5. Teach appreciation of the human body over other bodies. Pretend you are an elephant, bird, squirrel—what can you do? What can't you do? (Walk on two legs, pick up things with fingers, talk, walk while carrying something.) Now pretend you are a plant—what can't you do? (Almost everything.)

*6. Sensory stimulation. (a) Take a walk on a windy day. (b) Put a popcorn popper with no lid in the middle of a large, clean sheet or tablecloth on the floor. Watch and listen while the popping corn spews out like a fountain (see it, smell it, hear it, feel it, taste it). (c) Finger-paint with chocolate pudding. This also uses all five senses.

*7. Teach how the body moves. What parts of the body can open and close? What parts of the body can bend? Shake? Twist? Can you make a "T" with your body? an "E"? a "C"? (Some letters require two children to make their shapes.)

8. Relate the senses to their uses. Make a chart with six columns. List the five senses across the top of the chart in columns two through six. Let the children pick items to list down the left column and put checks in the appropriate columns for the senses that receive them. Examples: Wind—we hear it, feel it. A hot dog—we smell it, feel it, taste it, see it.

9. Talk about each activity afterward; recall it with glee. Say, "Wasn't it great to see which senses we use?" "Wasn't it fun to identify the sound?" Also, while the activity is actually taking place, try to find opportunities to say, "Isn't this fun?" "Aren't our bodies great?" (Note: This is a key throughout the process of teaching children joy. During and after each experience with joy, help the child to identify the joy and be conscious that he is feeling it, so that he wants it and recognizes it the next time.)

C. *Use and development of bodily skills.*

*1. Dancing and marching. Use a variety of music, ranging from light, fairylike ballet pieces to heavy soldier marches. The stronger the rhythm the better. Encourage freedom of movement and lack of inhibition: "Try to kick the ceiling." "Look like a big tree swaying in the breeze." Most children can feel the mood of music; encourage them to let it out. Sometimes a partially darkened room helps children to feel more free. Use a particularly free, uninhibited child as an example.

*2. Learning to catch a ball. Few abilities give a child a greater sense of physical confidence and satisfaction. A large foam or sponge ball is easy to catch, a good first step. Also, teach children to shoot a basket; both boys and girls need the feeling of physical prowess and ability. Again, use a sponge ball with a low basket. Teach them that missing is just fine; take it all lightly.

3. Provide small, manipulative toys—things that fit together and that develop hand-to-eye coordination. Puzzles—very simple ones at first—are good. Lavish praise for each right move: "Isn't that great? You are so good at it!" (But be careful not to tell children they are good if they are not; if they can't do it yet, they can't feel the joy yet. Say, "I'll bet you can do it when you are four. Now let's find something else.")

*4. Provide balancing toys, such as swing sets and tumbling mats. Encourage, but don't push, exploration, swinging, hanging, climbing, jumping off. Set up a simple obstacle course.

*5. Teach simple songs and offer the children praise for singing. Tape-record their music and let them have the joy of listening to it again.

Always give total encouragement and praise. A negative word can ruin fragile physical confidence and delay or thwart the very physical joy you are trying to create and teach. If the result is good, praise the result: "You did skip!" "You sang that right on tune!" If the result is not good, praise the attempt, the effort: "What a good try! Before long you'll do it!"

D. *Care of the body.*

1. Show children two cars: one clean and well cared for, with plenty of good gas and oil, and the other one broken down. Ask them which car they would rather have. Ask them how each owner took care of his car. Compare the cars to our bodies: gas and oil—good food; clean outside—regular baths; clean inside—brushed teeth; good tires—lots of exercise; bright headlights—enough sleep.

2. Show children pictures of two people: one an in-shape athlete, one a sagging, out-of-shape person. List the things one does that the other doesn't do: exercises, eats good food, keeps himself clean, gets enough sleep.

III. Family Focal Point: The Family Activity Board

There is something special about a family that does physical things together. There is something special about any relationship that is partially born out of shared physical activity. We learn when we play ball with someone, swim with someone; the activity brings the minds together, relaxes the atmosphere, and opens up the communication. This is doubly true in families. Families that play together stay together.

Our family has a list on a big, paper-covered bulletin board that we call "The Family Activity Board." Any family member, upon thinking of a physical or sports activity that he would like to do with the family, jots it down on the list with a big circle by it. Anticipation builds until a family home evening or free night comes along and allows the activity to happen. When it does, the circle is colored in.

We have defined what kinds of things can go on the board: things we can do together as a family that let our bodies stretch and exercise and feel good. Even the little ones understand. The list has become a rather interesting mixture of the conventional and the unconventional. It has included bowling, swimming, canoeing, sand-surfing at the dunes, walking to church instead of driving, bike riding all the way to Burke Lake, hiking in the Appalachians in the fall, using the stopwatch and having "records" for running around the block, and having Mom show us her yoga.

On one section of the activity board, we've put a "family records list"—the fastest time for running around the block, for skipping rope around the block. This charts the children's improvement and teaches the joy of progressing and excelling physically.

IV. Story: "Ben, the Rich Boy"

Once there was a boy named Ben. He was a strong and healthy lad. But he thought he was very, very poor because he had no money. When he saw people with money and fine things, it made him want to be rich.

Ben knew that there were four very rich men in the land. One day he decided that he would visit each of them and ask them how to be rich.

The first man lived on a hill in the northern part of the land. Ben asked him how to become rich. The man said, "Look out my window and tell me what you see." Ben looked out and saw beautiful red and orange leaves, because it was autumn. He saw blue sky, and purple, snow-capped mountains in the distance. He saw a hummingbird pausing at hollyhocks to collect honey. He told the man what he saw. "You are rich," said the man, "because of everything that your eyes can see." Ben left the first man's house. He wanted to be rich, and if that man wouldn't tell him how, he would find someone else who would.

The second rich man lived in a valley in the eastern part of the land. He was an old man with a long beard. Ben asked him how to become rich. The old man looked at Ben and said, "How did you get to my house?" "I walked from the north," said Ben. "Then you are rich," said the man. "You are rich because you have strong legs—you can walk and dance and skip and jump and run. I am old and lame. I would give every penny I have if I could walk like you." And Ben wondered why the man wouldn't tell him what he wanted to know.

Then Ben went to the third man's house, which was in a city in the southern part of the land. The man was out on his patio. Ben introduced himself and said, "Would you tell me how to become wealthy?" The man looked at Ben for a long time, then said, "Do you hear the crickets in my bush?" Ben said, "Yes." "Do you smell the food that is cooking?" "Yes," "Then you are rich. My senses are dim. I know of the sounds and smells only because I remember them. I cannot taste or feel or smell or hear as clearly as you. If I could, I would gladly give every penny I have."

Again Ben wondered why the man wouldn't tell him what he wanted to know.

The last man lived in a castle in the western part of the land. Ben went to him and said, "You are my last hope. Will you tell me how to be rich?" "But you must be rich," said the man. "Look at the fine shirt you wear." "This?" said Ben. "I had to make this shirt with my own hands and sew it with the thread made from the wool from my sheep." "Then you are rich. Your hands can make shirts and paint pictures and play musical instruments. My hands are old and shake so much that I can do none of these things. If I could, I would give every penny I have."

Ben left the man and started to go home. None of the men had told him how to be rich. All they had told him was that he was rich already because of his body and the things it could do. As Ben walked along, the sun shone warmly on his back and he heard the birds and animals around him and saw the flowers along his way. Perhaps he was rich. Maybe his body and the things he could be were worth more than money.

What do you think?

V. Reading List

Aliki. *My Five Senses.* New York: Thomas Y. Crowell Co., 1962.

Baylor, B. *Sometimes I Dance Mountains.* New York: Charles Scribner's Sons, 1973.

Bickerstaff, George. *My Body Is a Temple.* Salt Lake City: Bookcraft, 1978.

Ets, M. H. *Just Me.* New York: The Viking Press, 1967.

Gibson, M. *What Is Your Favorite Thing to Touch?* New York: Grosset & Dunlap, 1965.

Krauss, R. *The Growing Story.* New York: Harper & Row, 1947.

McGuire. *You, and How Your Body Works.* New York: Platt & Munk, 1974.

Merriam, E. *Andy All Year Round.* New York: Funk & Wagnalls, 1967.

Moncure, J. B. *About Me.* Chicago: Child's World, 1976.

Peterson, G. *Fun and Discovering with Your Five Senses.* Kansas City, Mo.: Hallmark Cards, 1977.

Showers, P. *Follow Your Nose.* New York: Thomas Y. Crowell Co., 1963.

Steiner, C. *Listen to My Seashell.* New York: Alfred A. Knopf, 1959.

Tudor, T. *First Delights.* New York: Platt & Munk, 1966.

Watson, J. W. *My Body, How It Works.* New York: Golden Press, 1972.

Records:

Brady, Janeen. *Watch Me Sing.* Salt Lake City: Brite Enterprises.

Hap Palmer Record Library, Educational Activities, Inc., Box 392, Freeport, N.Y.: *Creative Movement and Rhythm Expression* (AR 533); *Getting to Know Myself* (AR 543); *Learning Basic Skills through Music* (AR 514); *Movin'* (AR 546).

VI. Postscript

A. Julie's mother said she was hanging sheets on the line as four-year-old Julie handed her the clothespins. The sun was shining and a slight breeze was blowing. As a wet sheet blew against Julie, she grasped it with both hands and held it to her face. Then she stood back and looked at it and said, "This sheet looks so nice and clean. It smells good too, and it feels different when it's wet." Then she smiled and said, "I'm using some of my senses. I have five senses, but I can't hear the sheet or"—with a giggle, "I wonder what it tastes like."

B. As a group we were putting together a large puzzle of the body. As each child put on one part he would tell what it was for: eyes are to see with, knees are to bend. Becky, age three, whose mother had recently had twins, put on the arms and said, "I'm glad Heavenly Father made us with two arms so I can hug both my babies at the same time."

Teaching the Joy of the Earth 6

□ *The earth is the totally equipped laboratory for the "joy experiment." The raw materials are time and laws and agency. We are to turn these into joy.*

I. Examples and Description

A. *Adult:* Flat green, tilted mountainside darker greens, rocky mountaintop grays; I drink these in as the plane descends to land in Jackson Hole. Half an hour later I'm fishing in a clear brook. To my back stretches the soft, morning-lighted forest. Long, late-July grass carpets the ground below the large spruce; a smaller fir grows to my left. The downstream surface of the brook faintly flickers, reflecting light green trees at the back, dark green mountains in the middle, and blue sky in front of me.

Across the stream from me lies the Snake River Valley, and behind it, the Teton range. White, midsummer glaciers mark the crags and shaded spots in the jutting rock. A hawk floats, wing-tip feathers spread, across my field of vision. To my right, upstream, rise the Grand Tetons themselves, drawing the eye with an excitement that speeds the heart. They push through the only clouds in the sky. (A lonely cloud often sits there as if caught and held by the peaks.)

When I shut my eyes to make more of my brain available to my ears, I hear two ripples in the stream: one just upstream in my right ear and the other downstream in my left—stereophonic sound!

And the birds. I count five different kinds of chirps—only one that I know, the meadow lark: "Ain't I a pretty little bird?"

Once in a while a plane can be heard droning in the distance, and occasionally a cricket's rasp, behind and tucked between the other sounds.

One can't describe the smell. It combines so much—the grass, the trees, the sage—floating on air as clear and cool as the water in the stream. They seem so similar, the air and water: both clear, both cool, both fresh, both flowing (the current and the breeze).

I guess one reason I love Jackson so much is the seasons—the change, the transition, and the fact that, since I come only five or six times a year, the changes are distinct rather than gradual. One time (early summer) it will be like the day at the brook. Next time (early autumn) brings Indian summer when cottonwoods start to turn color, Snake River starts to turn clear, air starts to turn crisp, and sagebrush mountainsides look like scuffed buckskin against the sky's deeper blue. Next time it's late fall: the mantle of golden quaking aspen filters and softens the sun's more slanted rays. Flamelike cottonwoods pull forth the valley's deep purples and the cloud's fleecy white. The air is even crisper, almost tart. Then I come again in midwinter to ski; to sit alone in a soft snowstorm on a split-rail fence; to hear the silence of the white world; to see the fleecy, buffeting flakes building into quiet, white mounds around the darker, colder, half-ice streams; to feel the whole vibrant world settle and sleep.

There is such beauty in the earth. Joy comes through sensing it—with all five senses. I remember a poet I knew once, one who wrote mostly of the earth, who saw so much in the earth that I didn't see. He had a sign on his wall that said: "Five Sense Sagacity." I asked him about it. He said that serendipity, which means happy accidents, pleasant surprises, comes about through sagacity, which means acute awareness, appreciation, sensitivity, which in turn comes about through applied, thorough use of all five senses. Think about that for a moment; it is quite a message: "Happiness comes through awareness."

Joy and opportunity lie in the appreciation of the earth's beauties. So often we miss these joys—not because the earth lacks beauty (for indeed, every part of it is beautiful) but because of our apathy, our failure to see and to notice, our tendency to take it for granted.

B. *Child:* Our son Josh was fifteen months old and it was April. The summer before, he had been too small to be outside much, so, on this first nice day of the year, he was seeing the backyard for the first time. I watched him in silence from the window. He started with the grass, first feeling it, then sitting down in it, moving his legs back and forth, so delighted that he laughed aloud. Then he lay down, mouth open with an expression of anticipation, as he felt the grass with the back of his head and neck. From that position he noticed the sky and the clouds. He lifted both arms, pointed both forefingers, formed a round O with his little mouth, and said, with a tone of reverence and amazement, "Ooooooooohhh!" There was a spring breeze moving those fluffy clouds across the deep blue sky. He watched almost motionlessly for two or three minutes until the wind started to gust a little and he became more interested in the cool, feathery breeze on his skin. He stood up, turned his face into the breeze, squinted, gritted his teeth, and uttered his second descriptive sound, "Eeeeeeeeehhhhhhhh."

Turning in a new direction, he noticed a small patch of tiny white and yellow flowers in the grass. Toddling over, he reached down to pick one. The stem was fairly stiff, and as it broke, he fell back on his bottom into a sitting position. From there he held the flower close to his face and pulled off one tiny petal with his thumb and forefinger—a use of his hands he had recently discovered. When he had finished, he threw his little arms up, let the rest of the flower go at the top, and brought his hands slapping down on his knees with a contented sigh.

Then a bird chirped in the nearby tree. Josh cocked his head, a little startled, not sure where the sound had come from. The bird chirped again. This time Josh saw where it was. He stood up and toddled toward the tree. The bird swooped down, floated twenty yards or so, and landed on the lawn. Josh followed the flight with a look of delight

and utter amazement. As he watched, motionless, the bird
began his staccato pecking at the grass and an instant later
pulled up a squirming, wiggling worm. Josh shook his
head, as if in disbelief, and started shuffling toward the
bird. The bird fluttered back up into the tree, chirping all
the way.

Josh repeated his earlier cloud gesture, pointing up at
the bird with both hands and saying, "Ooooooooooh-
hhhhhh!"

II. Methods

A. *Teach the earth's terminology.*

1. Look together at large picture books of animals,
trees, and flowers. Point to a picture and have the children
say the name, or you say the name and have them point.

2. Point at things in nature wherever you go—point
and say the names.

3. Involve the children in picnics, nature walks, exposure to out-of-doors. At zoos or botanical gardens, or at
home in the backyard, notice nature. Talk about it; ask the
children to tell about it.

B. *Teach deep appreciation for the earth.*

1. Focus attention on one small sight or one small
sound. Have the children look through paper tubes (from
paper towels or toilet tissue) so they have one small field of
vision. Ask, "What do you see? Can you describe it? Isn't it
beautiful?" Now have the children close their eyes. Pick
out small, individual sounds and ask, "Can you hear that?"

*2. Use the senses chart again from the previous
chapter; however, this time focus attention on the things
from nature in the left vertical column rather than the
senses in the top horizontal column.

3. Take nature walks. You don't have to be in the
woods; a vacant field or a park will also do. Point out
things, but without too much explanation let the children
explore. If you find an ant hill, stop to watch. Ask what the

ants are doing. Ask lots of questions to help the child figure things out. Take nature walks to the same place in all four seasons, and ask: "How have things changed?"

*4. Put an ant colony in a glass case. The ants will make tunnels and the children can watch them work.

5. Teach children to distinguish nature from non-nature. On nature walks, ask them to find the things that are not nature's—cans, paper, litter—and pick them up. Point out that man's things are not as beautiful as God's; show that each little thing in nature is unique, while man's are often mass-produced.

*6. Make a visible "growing bottle." Put wet, crumpled paper towels in a bottle with seeds between the glass and the moist paper. Set it where it gets sunlight. Watch as roots grow down and leaves and shoots grow up.

7. Watch ants and bugs with the children and be interested in them instead of smashing them.

8. Paste up a collage from each season. Look through magazines together for pictures: "Here's something for winter—here are pictures of autumn leaves for fall."

*9. Make four-season collections—nature things picked up from each season. Gather autumn seeds and grain from fall, flowers from spring, bare branches from winter.

10. Watch and feed birds.

11. Have pets. Learn about them and how to take care of them. Some areas have pet libraries where children can check out a pet for a week.

12. Listen to classical music and tell what things from nature your mind sees as you listen.

13. Take pictures of beautiful things the children point out—or let them snap their own pictures. Enjoy the experiences again when you see the prints or slides.

14. Expose children to the arts. Take them to galleries, to concerts, to museums.

   C. *Teach the joys of the use of nature.*

*1. Get a small, simple loom to make cloth from wool.

*2. Milk a cow, drink the milk, make butter, gather eggs, and cook them.

*3. Gather wheat, take the chaff off yourself, grind the wheat, make dough, bake bread.

*4. Play a question and answer game about the uses of nature: "What can you do or make with a tree? with sand? with a cow?"

*5. Have a nature meal, with honey, eggs, milk, and home-baked bread.

6. Walk through the supermarket and see if the children can tell where different foods come from and how nature provides them. Walk by clothing displays and have them tell you the same things about the cloth.

III. Family Focal Point: The Family Favorite Things Wall

About the time our Saren turned three, her artistic talents becoming more manifest each day, she took to drawing on the walls. We tried various means to dissuade her from this practice, but our efforts were tempered by the creativity and beauty of her "artwork" and by the fact that she seemed to have far more interest in the walls than in paper, blackboard, or anything else we could provide.

Finally, in desperation, we designated one wall in the den, where nobody but our family goes, for drawing on. It consequently became known as the drawing room. Saren confined her efforts to that wall and, before long, its lower half was covered with faces and shapes of all description.

Not long after this, we held a family home evening on "favorite things." We were thinking of the small, simple things in life that give us pleasure: snowflakes, kites, crackling fires, the opening day of fishing season, single roses, the sound of crisp apples being dumped into a box, the sound of the woodpecker behind our house. The list kept growing, but we had nowhere to put it except on that wall.

Since that night we've called it the "favorite things wall." Whenever someone notices something he enjoys, something that gives him a small spark of pure joy, he writes it on the wall, thus sharing it and, through sharing, remembering it. (Children who are too young to write can draw their favorite thing.) The wall became so valuable to us over the years that when we rented the house to someone else, we included in the rental agreement a clause prohibiting any redecorating or painting over those favorite things.

IV. Story: "Earth Ernie"

Ernie was playing alone one day in his backyard with a little dump truck and a steam shovel. All at once he heard a whirling noise, and when he looked up, he saw a purple, round spinning thing that looked like a big plate. Ernie knew that it was a spaceship. (He had seen pictures.)

A hatch in the bottom opened, and out came a small purple man. Ernie knew right away that he was friendly, because he was smiling. "Hi," said Ernie, because he was friendly too. When the purple man said, "Hello, Ernie," it made Ernie think of two questions. One was, "How did you know my name?" and the other was, "How do you know how to speak English?" The little purple man said it was because he had been listening from his planet through his "ear telescope," which made faraway sounds easy to hear. "I came to see you," said the little purple man, "because you are one of the nicest people I've listened to. I'd like you to come for a ride with me to my planet. Our king is too old to travel, and he would like to meet an earth person."

"Well," said Ernie, "I sure would like to ride in your flying saucer and see your world, but my mother would worry about me."

"No, she won't," said the little purple man. "My spaceship goes faster than time, so I can have you right back here in your backyard before she even knows you've gone."

Well, Ernie didn't exactly understand that, but he surely did want to ride in that flying saucer, so he pretended he understood and climbed in behind the little purple man.

The ride was fun. Ernie got to drive the spaceship part of the way. It had a steering wheel like a car. The ship went very fast, and once the little purple man, who told Ernie his name was Thoyd, had to take the steering wheel because Ernie nearly hit a star.

Before long the ship slowed down, and Ernie could see a very round, very flat, very shiny purple world. "There's my planet," said Thoyd. "Isn't it pretty?" "Yes," said Ernie, "so shiny and flat." "It's made out of purple plastic," said Thoyd. "Plastic?" said Ernie. "Yes, we made it," said Thoyd. "We used to have a world like yours, but the air and water got so dirty and there was so much garbage everywhere that we had to make ourselves this new one."

"But where are your trees and your animals, Thoyd?"

"Oh, we don't have those things anymore. They don't grow on plastic. We have synthetic food. It comes in six flavors and looks a little like toothpaste."

"But do you have any mountains to climb or lakes to float in?"

"No," said Thoyd, "we lost those too, but this purple plastic world is great for roller skating." Thoyd went to get the king, and Ernie looked around. The air smelled like plastic. There were no flowers or grass, no fields or hills or rocks, no sounds of birds or babbling brooks or wind in the trees; there were no farm animals or cold milk or fresh eggs; no ears of corn to pick or potatoes to dig; not even any sand or soil. The blue sky didn't look as pretty as it should next to the shiny purple horizon.

Pretty soon Thoyd came back with a very old-looking little purple man who had a purple plastic crown and a long beard. Thoyd said, "This is King Pele. He is the only purple man old enough to remember our old world—and he has a message for you." The old king came up close to Ernie, held Ernie's hand, and leaned his mouth close to Ernie's ear. "Earth Ernie," said the old king in a faint, gruff whisper, "tell your people to know and love their earth, or they will lose it like we lost ours." The old king patted Ernie's shoulder and smiled at him; then he slowly walked away.

"Do you want to stay and have a tour of our world?" asked Thoyd. "No, thanks," said Ernie. He just wanted to get back to his beautiful earth to make sure it was still there. "I understand," said Thoyd, and they got back on the flying saucer.

They seemed to go slower on the way back, and Ernie wanted to get back so badly. Finally they landed in his backyard and, just as Thoyd had said, Ernie's mother was still inside and everything was just as they had left it.

As soon as Thoyd was gone, Ernie ran to get his mother and his little sister, Sue. "Come," he said, taking each of their hands. "Where are we going, Ernie?" "To the park," said Ernie. For the next hour, Ernie showed his mother the trees and grass, the flowers and bushes. They smelled roses, patted dogs, listened to every sound that nature made, and even picked up every scrap of litter they could find.

"We need to love our world, Mommy. Otherwise we'll lose it." Mother didn't know what had gotten into Ernie, but she agreed with him anyway.

V. Reading List

Bulla, C. *A Tree Is a Plant.* New York: Thomas Y. Crowell Co., 1960.

Cornelius, C. *Isabella Wally Bear Tiger Moth.* Chicago Child's World, 1978.

Ets, M. H. *Gilberto and the Wind.* New York: The Viking Press, 1963.

Keats, E. J. *The Snowy Day.* New York: Viking Press, 1962.

Merriam, E. *Andy All Year Round.* New York: Funk & Wagnalls, 1967.

Moncure, J. *Fall Is Here.* Chicago: Child's World, 1976.

_____. *Spring Is Here.* Chicago: Child's World, 1976.

_____. *Summer Is Here.* Chicago: Child's World, 1976.

_____. *Thank You, Animal Friends.* Chicago: Child's World, 1975.

_____. *What Will It Be?* Chicago: Child's World, 1976.

_____. *Winter Is Here.* Chicago: Child's World, 1976.

Parr, L. *When Sea and Sky Are Blue.* New York: Scroll Press, 1971.

Paull, G. *Come to the Country.* New York: Abelard Schuman, 1956.

Provensen, A., and Provensen, M. *A Book of Seasons.* New York: Random House, 1976.

Ranger Rick's Nature Magazine. National Wildlife Federation (12 issues per year), 1412 16th St. N. W., Washington, D.C., 20036.

Shulevitz, U. *Rain, Rain, Rivers.* New York: Farrar, Straus, & Giroux, 1969.

Tudor, T. *Five Senses.* New York: Platt & Munk, 1978.

Udry, J. M. *A Tree Is Nice.* New York: Harper & Row Publishers, 1956.

Watson, J. W. *Wonders of Nature.* New York: Golden Press, 1958.

VI. Postscript

A. Matthew is nearly five. His mother said the family had gone on a picnic for family home evening and Matthew kept calling everyone's attention to the mountains, the trees, the clouds, the wind, and so forth, saying, "That's part of our beautiful world." By the time they were ready to go home, he had gathered several things in a plastic bag to take with him. He had a large pinecone, a smooth stone, a wild flower, a bur, and a dead beetle. He wanted to share part of nature, he said, with the old man who lived next door.

B. According to his mother, David, age three, has started talking to the animals and trees. One day he gave the apple tree a friendly pat and said, "Thank you for the apples." As he watched a bee buzzing around the flowers, he said, "Thank you, bee, for the honey." And as they drove along a country road past a field of cows, he called out, "Thank you for the milk, cows, and for the butter and ice cream too."

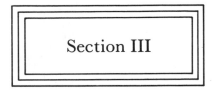

Section III

MENTAL JOYS

"Our home joys are the most delightful earth affords, and the joy of parents in their children is the most holy joy of humanity. It makes their hearts pure and good; it lifts them up to their Father in heaven." (Johann Heinrich Pestalozzi.)

Preserving the Joy of Interest and Curiosity 7

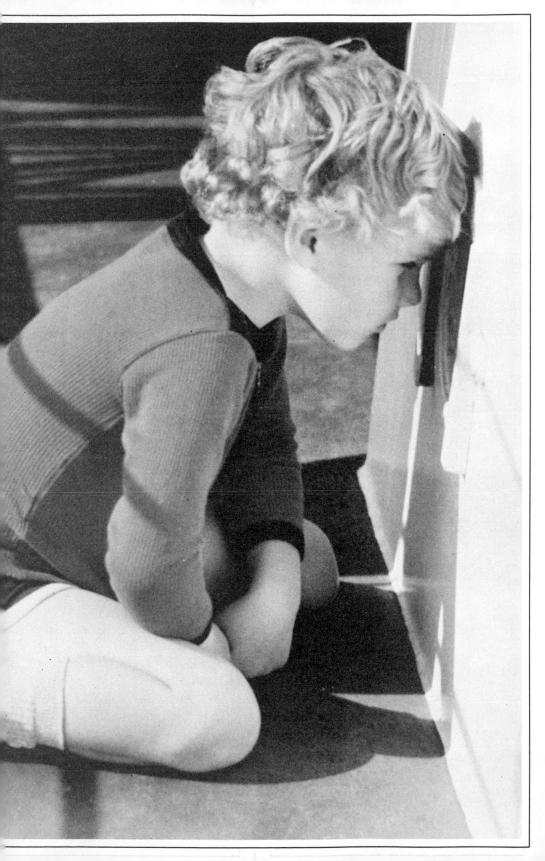

☐ *Ah, to see the world through the eyes of a child, where there is wonder in all things and where boredom or routine do not exist.*

I. Examples and Description

A. *Child:* I remember sitting once, off to the side in a busy shopping mall, looking at passing people—watching to see who was watching. The adults were preoccupied with their jobs, their problems, themselves. Their eyes never met mine. Their eyes saw only what was necessary to navigate through the crowded corridor.

But the little children saw everything. Each child looked straight at me for at least a moment, and for a moment at everything. Their eyes and ears were receptors, taking in all the data, seeing, hearing, questioning.

It is no wonder that we learn as much in our first five years as in the rest of our lives. We see more, feel more. We are born with a natural and joyful curiosity and interest. What happens to it? Where did those adults drop it? When would those children lose theirs?

One study showed that babies spend one-fifth of their waking hours in motionless, focused gazing, simply figuring things out with their eyes. Their minds are so malleable, so impressionable! Parents can perhaps change their children's minds more, for better or for worse, than they can change either their bodies or their spirits.

B. *Adult:* I had been a student in Boston for two years. I loved the city and thought I knew it pretty well. Then a visitor came to spend a weekend with us on his way through the city. "What do you want to do?" I asked. "See Boston!" he said. I took him to my favorite places: the Wharf, Hay Market Square, the Freedom Trail. His eyes were wide the whole day. His comments were of fascination, even awe. "That really happened here?" His questions were questions of genuine interest, questions of history, of geography, of personality, of joyful curiosity. I couldn't answer most of them because I had never asked them. In those two days I think I saw more reflected in his eyes than I had seen in two years through my own eyes.

I thought I loved Boston, but my friend enjoyed the tour, enjoyed the day, the people, the smells, the feelings, more than I had the first time I had seen them or at any time since. The joy that I saw in his face was the involved, absorbed, wrapped-up, forget-himself-and-his-own-problems joy of curiosity and of interest. He had, preserved within him, a joy that nearly all small children possess and nearly all adults lose.

II. Methods

A. *Learn from children's example; participate with and encourage them.* My wife and I observed our three-year-old through the back window playing alone among the flowers on a warm, early-spring day. Her delight and intense interest showed so clearly that we felt it, and I murmured, "How can we keep that in her forever?" My wife replied, "By watching her watching, and watching what she watches."

Since then, we have come to know that that's the secret. Children are the teachers, the experts; we are the learners, the students. The teachers can be encouraged by the interest of the learners, and thus their interest-expertise can gain the element of pride that causes it to remain. Changes for application come daily: instead of pulling them away from their activity (jumping in leaves) and into yours (cleaning the house), how about occasionally leaving *yours* to join them in *theirs*? (Don't worry, the leaves will brush out of your hair.)

B. *Answer and ask.* While you are in those leaves, your teacher (your child) may ask, "Did a caterpillar make this hole in this leaf?" You might consider three responses: thanking him for teaching you to have an interest in that hole; answering him by saying, "Yes, a caterpillar probably did"; and opening a chance for more teaching by asking, "And where do you suppose that caterpillar is right now?"

How precious a question is! An alert mind that asks is the first step to answers, discoveries, solutions. Never ignore or criticize a question; this is like stepping on a flower bud just set to bloom. The moment a question is asked is like the moment a flower blooms on an early spring morning. The air is clean and crisp, the images precise and distinct. The child's mind is ready to absorb; the moment won't last. So many people—running, hurrying, preoccupied— walk past the flower, drive right through the spring morning without seeing or smelling it, and the moment passes, forever lost. The child asks and we defer, brush off, hurry the answer, or, even worse, say, "Don't bother me now, I'm busy." Oh, the need to go the other direction—to praise the question, to flatter him for asking it, to help a child glory in his wonderings!

Actually, to go back to the analogy, two mistakes are commonly made as the flower blooms on the new spring morning. One is to miss it, walk past it, never see it; the other is to *pick* it instead of appreciating it, enjoying it, helping if we can to make it grow.

With a questioning child, one of two similar mistakes usually occurs: (1) ignoring, brushing off, not noticing the beauty and potential of that moment, and (2) answering instead of reasoning together, helping, or asking questions of the child that will help him answer his own. When we take the time to discuss a question, we help the child to understand the wonderful concepts of reasoning, conceptualizing, researching—the ideas that allow him to glory in his wonderings and rejoice in discovered answers.

C. *Respond to your child's initiative.* A well-documented Harvard study reveals something few would expect: that parents of the smartest children don't try to teach them all the time, but try to teach only when the child wants to learn. The study took students from apparently similar backgrounds, all from good families, upper-middle-class homes, nonworking mothers, with no apparent hereditary differences and no apparent emotional differences. One subgroup had high I.Q.s and high grades, while the other had lower grades and lower I.Q.s. The object of the study was to determine where the difference first occurred, where the smart got smart and vice versa.

The researchers went back a year at a time, looking for differences. They didn't find any until they got to the preschool years at home. The difference was the mothers. Mothers of the high I.Q. and good-grade children (the "A" mothers) were *consultants*. They loved their children, but they let them develop in their own way. They gave freedom, an interesting environment, and time, but not all their time. They had a wide variety of other interests besides their children. They painted, they took violin lessons, or they played tennis, but they recognized teaching moments and taught what their children were interested in *when* they were interested in it. They gave the initiative to their children.

The "C" mothers overtaught, overprotected, and oversupervised their children and did their thinking for them. They constantly tried to teach things—with or without their children's interest. They were *managers* rather than *consultants*. Their children were long on fear and timidness, short on initiative, confidence, and self-reliance.

The "A" mothers organized and designed stimulating, open environments for children, with a rich variety of toys and household objects. Nothing was off-limits or "no no." Dangerous things were removed, and the child was free.

The "C" mothers actually spent more time with children, had fewer other interests, but their time was spent *managing* the child, force-teaching him, programming him. The "C" children were spoiled. They saw little fulfillment and excitement in the adulthood their mothers mirrored. They did not learn to struggle, to solve problems, to decide, or to take initiative.

Perhaps the saddest part of the Harvard study is that the "C" mothers thought they were doing so well. They were conscientious, diligent, and sacrificing. They thought they were putting their child's welfare above their own. The "A" mothers, consciously or subconsciously, realized that children have the joy of interest and curiosity and that the gift is best cultivated by encouraging initiative, by giving freedom, and by answering and teaching primarily when questions come.

The "A" mothers seemed to realize that ten minutes with a child when he asks, when he wants the time, may be more valuable than several hours when the parent has the time but the child is not interested.

D. *Stimulation.* The child's interest and curiosity behave a little like a beast of prey: as long as it finds enough food in its environment, as long as it is not starved, it continues to prowl. If a child gets enough stimulation, enough answers, enough of his parents' time when he wants that time, his interest and curiosity will flourish and grow and will continue to be the windows that open his mind to joy.

This principle applies even to very small children. As soon as babies can see, they need visual stimulation: mobiles, bright colors, moving objects to observe. Parents should show them things, talk to them, give their new eyes and arms and bodies chances to see and hear and feel widely different things.

*E. *"Interest" games.* These include simple question-and-answer games; simple science experiments with such things as water, air, magnets, and gravity (ask: "What will happen . . ."); simple magic tricks.

*F. *"Interest" stories.* Read and tell stories that excite children and make them anxious to see what happens, stories with suspense, mystery, or surprise.

G. *Research.* If you have access to a good set of encyclopedias, teach children that nearly all questions have answers, that it is good to ask and fun to find. Spend time in libraries. Teach children where the various sections are, and how they can find books on particular subjects, things they can understand. Be excited when they discover something themselves.

*H. *Early academic skill.* As is obvious to the reader by

now, the whole direction of this book is away from forced, early academic skills, against the idea of pushing three- and four-year-olds to learn their basic reading and number skills a year or two early, against using these incredible impressionable years in teaching something as ordinary as the academic skills that they will spend the next twelve years learning anyway.

But there is another side of the coin that cannot go unnoticed. A child's academic confidence, which will largely determine how well he does in his twelve or more years of formal schooling, is largely framed in his earliest school experiences—kindergarten and first grade. A child who senses that he is behind, that some of his peers can read words and write numbers and he cannot, may suffer an academic self-image deflation that is hard and time-consuming to overcome. There are two fairly straightforward ways to avoid this:

1. Tell the five-year-old that some children have had early reading or writing or numbers instruction, that they will naturally know more at first, but not to worry because "You will soon catch up." Go a step further and tell the five-year-old that he has been busy learning other things, about his body and about the earth and about other happy things that are most important. Tell him that now the time has come for school, and that he will catch up to those who started that kind of schooling earlier.

2. Three or four months before school starts, teach the five-year-old some basic school-related skills that will give him early confidence. By then he will be curious about school and will have questions that will make him attentive and anxious to learn some basic academic skills.

The following checklist represents what a child ought to be able to do before his first day of school in order to start off with basic confidence. Your child will already know many things on the list, through the natural consequences of growing up and of being curious and asking. The others can easily be taught in the months immediately preceding school.

Shapes
> Trace a line of shapes
> Copy shapes and a series of shapes
> Match shapes and equal numbers of shapes
> Identify shapes
> Recognize shapes in familiar objects
> Recognize by name and be able to draw circles, squares, triangles, and rectangles

Colors
> Match basic colors
> Identify basic colors
> Describe colors by name
> Relate colors to familiar objects

Letters
> Trace and copy letters
> Remember order of three letters
> Connect matching letters
> Match letters
> Recognize letters in own name
> Print own name (lowercase except first initial)

Numbers
> Trace and copy numbers
> Identify written numbers up to ten
> Compare larger-smaller numbers by circling largest amount of object, saying or choosing largest number, or indicating what comes before or after a given number
> Count to 20
> Relate groups of objects to numbers
> Know phone number and street address

III. *Family Focal Point: The Family Interest Book*

Children who are made to feel proud of their interest and curiosity quickly want to share what they have noticed. If there is a way or vehicle by which they can share the discoveries or fruits of their curiosity and interest, then that vehicle, that chance to share, becomes an additional motivation to continue to be curious and interested.

In our family, we have an "interest book," not for finances or money, but for *interest* interest. It is nothing more than a simple, hardbound book of blank paper in which any family member can make note of something interesting that he has observed or discovered. Preschoolers, of course, tell a grownup to write in their observations. Reading back through that interest book is a joy:

"A blue and black bird is building a nest in the tree by the corner of the house." (Saren, age four.)

"Barney (our dog) can get over to his friend's house because there is a hole in the fence where it goes behind the shed." (Shawni, age three.)

"When you kick a rock so it bounces across the patio, it makes a hollow sound." (Daddy.)

"The reason robins stand so still before they peck for a worm is that they are *listening* to know where the worm is— they can hear the worm—that's why they cock their heads." (Saren, age five.)

Our interest book hangs on a hook in the family room. We are aware of it, so we like to share in it. Every month or so, in a family home evening, we read all the entries that have been made. Like certain other types of interest books, ours grows in value with the passage of time.

IV. Story: "Maisey and Daisey"

Maisey and Daisey were squirrels, and they were sisters. Maisey was more the hurrying type, while Daisey was more the curious type. One day they were walking to school and they remembered that it was their teacher's birthday. "I wish it were later in the year and the flowers were blooming," said Maisey. "We could bring her a bouquet!" "Well, there are some flowers blooming," said Daisey. "I saw them yesterday just down from the bridge over the creek." (Daisey, you see, noticed nearly everything.)

So off the girls went to the bridge. Maisey was hurrying

to get there, but Daisey was noticing while they were walking. She noticed a big, hollow tree and a red ribbon someone had dropped, and she noticed that it was getting rather windy and cloudy.

They found the flowers and picked them. "Oh, if we only had something to hold them together," said Maisey. Daisey held up the red ribbon she had found. It was perfect. They tied the stems of the flowers together and started back for school.

Daisey was still noticing the wind and the clouds, and when they came to the big, hollow tree, she said, "Maisey, it's going to rain. If we go on, we'll get very wet. But if we get in this big, hollow tree, we can stay dry until the rain stops." It was a very good idea, and that's exactly what they did.

The rain didn't last long, and they soon came out, nice and dry, with a dry bouquet of flowers and a dry ribbon. Maisey looked at her sister Daisey and said, "If it weren't for you noticing everything so well, we wouldn't have any flowers for our teacher. And even if we had flowers, we wouldn't have a ribbon. And even if we had flowers and a ribbon, they would have all been spoiled and we would have been spoiled if you hadn't noticed that tree. I'm going to try to notice more things as you always do."

That made Daisey happy, and they put their arms around each other's shoulders and skipped off to school.

V. Reading List

Aliki. *Is It Blue as a Butterfly?* New York: Prentice Hall, 1965.

Epstein, S., and Epstein, B. *Grandpa's Wonderful Glass.* New York: Grosset & Dunlap, 1962.

Ford, B. G. *Do You Know?* New York: Random House, 1979.

Goudey, A. E. *The Day We Saw the Sun Come Up.* New York: Charles Scribner's Sons, 1961.

Hoban, R. *Herman the Loser.* New York: Harper & Row Publishers, 1961.

Johnson, D. *Stop, Look and Listen.* Cincinnati: Standard Publishing Co., 1977.

Moncure, J. *Riddle Me a Riddle.* Chicago: Child's World, 1977.

_____. *What Causes It?* Chicago: Child's World, 1977.

Odor, R. *My Wonder Book.* Chicago: Children's Press, 1977.

Polgreen, J., and Polgreen, C. *Good Morning Mr. Sun.* New York: Holt, Rinehart & Winston, 1963.

Rand, A., and Rand, P. *I Know a Lot of Things.* New York: Harcourt, Brace & Co., 1956.

Schwartz, J. *Now I Know.* New York: McGraw Hill, 1955.

Tobias, T. *Where Does It Come From?* Chicago: Children's Press, 1977.

Wyler, R. *What Happens If?* (Science experiments you can do by yourself). New York: Scholastic Book Services, 1974.

Zolotow, C. *When the Wind Stops.* New York: Harper & Row Publishers, 1975.

VI. *Postscript*

Jason, age four and a half: "Teacher, yesterday I did the same things as that little boy in the story you read us."

Teacher: "What story was that, Jason?"

Jason: "You know. The one about the boy who kept his eyes and ears open during the day to find out what made all the noises he would hear after he went to bed at night. Well, I did that too, and now I know."

Teacher: "That's great, Jason."

Jason: "And guess what that scary noise is that I hear every night."

Teacher: "What is it?"

Jason: "Just the lady upstairs rocking in her rocking chair."

Teaching the Joy of Imagination and Creativity 8

☐ *If one can imagine, he can create. If he can create, he can make the world a better place. Imagination is the first spark that ignites the flame of fulfillment.*

I. Examples and Description

A. *Adult:* I remember once in college when Linda gave me a glimpse of the joy of imagination and creativity. I called her one crisp autumn Saturday morning to see if we could spend the day together. She said, "Sure, but let me plan what we do this time." I agreed. She said, "Come on over, and wear old clothes." We knew each other well but were not yet engaged.

When I got there, she came out with an assortment of sketch pads, paints, and brushes. "But I can't paint," I said. "Neither can I," she said. "I borrowed these from my roommate."

Under her direction, I drove toward the mountains. It was a clear, tingling day, with the sky a deep autumn blue. We wound higher into a flame-colored canyon; the red scrub oak and yellow aspen set the steep slopes on fire and made them somehow higher, vaster, so that they towered all around and almost over us. It was like driving through a tunnel of flame, with the cool blue and grey strips of sky and road just above and just below.

We turned onto a dirt road and wound upward until we came to a deserted cabin perched among the bright leaves. We set up our easels on the big front porch. I remember, looking down from there, that the hillside seemed alive, each round yellow aspen leaf quivering and rotating in the soft breeze. She said, "Now, make believe that you are a great artist." Her eyes sparkled with interest as she prepared to imagine the same thing.

She got into it faster than I did. Her brush strokes were big and bold, as though she'd painted all her life. She said, "Imagine that we just landed here from another planet. What would we think of this earth? What would we think of the town when we drove into it?" In spite of myself, I let her talk me into the discussion. We imagined as children do. We felt the joy and abandon of letting our minds go unshackled. I did more creating that day—with brush and mind—than I can remember in years before or since, and I was a better person for it—more light, more alive, more feeling. There was a certain wonder, a certain power, a certain joy.

B. *Child:* Several years later, after marriage and family, I came in the back door one afternoon, quietly, getting home from work early. Before anyone heard me, I heard my two girls, ages five and four, in their bedroom.

"All right, I'll be the doctor if you'll be the nurse."

"Okay."

"Now if we can get Barney (the dog) to stay under these covers, then he can be the sick guy."

"Yeah, and this stick can be for the operation." (I restrained my urge to defend the poor dog.)

"We'd better put the sick guy to sleep before the operation."

"These can be the sleep pills."

"Oh, but Barney won't close his eyes. I better sing him a song—then he can stay awake and it won't hurt. Oh sick guy, sick guy, you have such a big long tongue, we will do your operation and you'll look better and feel better too." (The tune was kind of a mixture between Mary Poppins and a Sunday School song; the words rambled on for several "verses.")

Later that week, at bedtime one night, I asked the five-year-old to tell me a bedtime story for a change. It was an incredible story that introduced two new animals to the earth: a "Caxton," a round animal with fur and no feet because it rolls along, and a "Sarapoo," a little animal with long ears like a bunny that has such shaggy hair that it can't see. We (Saren and I) later made an illustrated book of the story.

Children's minds are the most free, the most creative, the least bound by inhibition and tradition. Therefore, it's

easy to teach them creativity and imagination. Unfortu-
nately, it is also dangerously easy to say "that's silly," or
"grow up," or "quit imagining things." It is an interesting
paradox that the times when parents usually tell their
children to be grown-up are the times when the children
are having the most fun, feeling the most joy. Do we really
want them to grow up, or would we do better to "grow
down," to be more like they are—more free, more imagina-
tive, less inhibited?

There is power in imagination. One who can imagine
himself doing something gets that much closer to actually
doing it.

There is safety in imagination. One who can imagine
the future may avoid "future shock" when he gets there.

There is youth in imagination, and children should
know from us, through us, that they will never get too old
to imagine.

A child who imagines will become an adult who
creates, who solves problems with lateral thinking and with
innovative solutions; who will see the less obvious, do the
less common, find the more unusual. A child who imagines
being an adult will become an adult with less pain and less
adjustment. Imagination is the magic "learning tunnel"
that sometimes lets us learn without actually experiencing.

Too many of us think of imagination as impractical or
irrelevant. Actually, in a world where children grow up to
be engineers, consultants, computer operators, and perhaps
many other things that you and I haven't yet dreamed of,
imagination may be the best and most practical training
they could have.

Oh, how children love it when they find that their
parents have imaginations! I went up to tuck the two little
girls in bed one night after shoveling the snow from the
front walk. I still had on my big, white furry coat, so I
pulled the hood down over my face and announced myself
as "Polar Bear," come from the North Pole to tell a
bedtime story. Since then, Polar Bear just has to come back

once a month or so—alternating with other characters made up from very slight disguises and very big imaginations.

II. Methods

A. *The old standby: liberal encouragement.* Give enormous encouragement for the slightest show of creativity—from building with blocks to drawing a picture. Watch as though a masterpiece were being unveiled.

Sometimes encouragement involves more than just words. It may involve providing reams of scratch paper for the three-year-old to make pictures on. Often we tend to think of this as a waste because that's what our parents or teachers taught us, when in reality the child is creating something on each sheet and even possibly improving just a bit by being allowed to experiment. Though I have to bite my lip as I say this, as only recently I scolded my four-year-old for using practically a whole roll of sticky tape to get an old piece of Christmas paper to stick to his door, it's worth thirty-nine cents to have him feel he has really accomplished something. On closer examination, I found that he had been very meticulous and had covered every square inch of the paper with the tape.

B. *The other old standby: being a child with them.* When they imagine, we imagine. Play in the mud with them for a change. Don't inhibit through restricting any more than is absolutely necessary.

*C. *Seeing in the mind.* Listen to classical music with children. Close your eyes and see whatever the music makes you see. Describe it vividly: "horses with fine ladies and parasols, trotting on the green on a clear summer day." Ask the children to do the same.

*D. *Making things.*

1. Whip up soap flakes with an eggbeater. Put the mixture on construction paper and let the children mold it, then let it dry. Praise and compliment and ask about each creation. (Don't insult a child by asking "What is it?" Instead say "Tell me about it.")

2. Don't buy things ready-made when you can buy kits or make them from scratch. Think of ways to make musical instruments (rhythm blocks, scrapers) and other simple, useful things.

3. Throw away the Tinker Toy instructions and let children figure out their own construction.

4. Make things from nature—necklaces from dandelion stems, daisy chains, and so forth.

E. *Pretending.*

*1. Save old dresses, shoes, and hats in a box or chest for dress-up clothes. What treasures they can be to an active imagination!

*2. Pretend that inanimate objects and body parts can talk: food that wants to be in the tummy, toys that want to be played with, ears that want to be washed.

3. Pretend to be little elves who come and clean up the toys; then pretend to be the little children who are surprised to find their room cleaned up.

4. Have imaginary friends who come to play.

*5. Dramatize children's favorite stories.

F. *Solving problems.*

*1. Have a hand puppet whisper in a child's ear an indistinguishable "psst psst." Let the child decide what he thinks the puppet said. Children will often talk with less inhibition when speaking for a puppet than when speaking for themselves.

*2. Play the "how else could he have done that" game. Examples: How could we get a chair over here without carrying it? (Tie a rope on it and drag it.) How could we get a marble from under the sofa? (With a stick.) How could we keep the tablecloth down at a picnic on a windy day? (With rocks.) How could we carry many things at once? (In pockets, in a box.)

G. *Stories and games.*

1. Try role reversal. Let the children be the parents and put you to bed, or get you to eat your dinner. They

will learn a bit about adulthood and will likely perform their roles better as children in the future.

2. Let them fill in the blanks of your story, thus letting their minds chart the direction of the story.

*3. Tell them a story with a not-so-happy ending; then tell it again and let them change the ending to make it happier.

*4. Have hand puppets act out stories or situations; let the children wear the puppets.

H. *Creating through the ear.*

*1. Try creative dance. Put on classical music and different kinds of other good music and let your body move the way the music wants it to.

2. Sing together in the car. Children can sing simple harmony parts early if helped properly. Especially use "joy-producing" tunes.

*3. Have a rhythm band with simple instruments and marching.

*4. Play "once upon a time, I caught a little rhyme. I put it on the mat and it turned into a _____. I put it on my bed and it jumped up on my _____," etc.

I. *Creating through the eye.*

1. Fingerpaint or footpaint; let a creative mess be made.

2. Bring out crayons, tempera paints, and watercolor markers, and paint together as a family. Praise each painting as unique and good, none better than the other. Provide the medium, then let the children use their own ideas.

3. Play with clay or dough—sometimes with tools, but usually with hands only. Don't tell children what to make; let them create. Here's a quick play dough recipe: Mix together in a pot 1 cup flour, 1 tablespoon oil, 1 cup water, ½ cup salt, 2 teaspoons cream of tartar, and a few drops of food coloring. Cook over medium heat, stirring constantly, until dough pulls away from the pot's sides and forms a ball. The cooking takes only about thirty seconds. Remove

from heat and knead about ten times until dough is smooth. Store in a plastic bag. This makes a soft, smooth dough that will dry out, but not enough to make things like jewelry. If kept in a plastic bag in the refrigerator, it will stay soft for several months.

*4. Observe nature and ask children if they can find any place where nature made two things exactly the same. Compare with "sameness" of man-made things.

J. *Combining creativity and imagination* (more obviously than they are usually combined).

1. Write a book together. Let the child think of the story and illustrate it while you put in the words. Saddle-stitch it with staples, making it sturdy and as much like a real book as you can. Let the child develop the characters and plot. Put the child's name on the front cover as the author.

*2. Show a picture. Have a child make up a story about what's happening in the picture.

*3. Give a child varied materials: styrofoam, toothpicks, pipe cleaners, colored paper, feathers, scissors, and glue, and let him make his own creation.

*4. Produce an 8mm movie together—let the children be the producer, director, cameraman, and actors. Make anything from a role-played fairy tale to a documentary on nature, such as "Signs of Spring." Do a cassette tape for the soundtrack. Invite friends over to see the finished production.

*5. Make a radio show on a tape recorder. Do the sound effects and have a moderator and characters. Invite friends over to listen to the story.

III. Family Focal Point: The Mommy-Daddy Proud Board

One Saturday, four-year-old Saren was "helping" me recarpet a room. We talked for a while as I worked; then I got involved and lost track of her for a few moments. Soon she tapped my shoulder and squealed delightedly, "Look

Dad, a boat!" She had found two sail-shaped scraps and one boat-shaped scrap and stuck them together with the carpet backing. It really did look like a sailboat, and I made a fuss over her creativity.

Then Saren wanted a special place to display her boat. Mommy dug out an old bulletin board and we hung it in the family room with Saren's boat pinned right in the center. Within ten minutes, two-year-old Shawni had drawn two pictures and with her limited vocabulary was demanding equal billing.

That night Saren dubbed the bulletin board "The Mommy-Daddy Proud Board." It's never been off the wall since. The drawings and colorings and creations of all kinds stay up until new ones take their place, at which point they come down and go directly into the scrapbook. Children, like all artists, need appreciation and praise to fuel their creative fires.

IV. Story: "Epamanatus"

Epamanatus lived with his mother in a little house in the village. One day his mother said, "Epamanatus, you are old enough to go to the store for me." So Epamanatus went to the store, and he took along his little puppy. On the way home, the puppy ran away and was lost for nearly three hours. When the little puppy got home again, Epamanatus's mother said, "Epamanatus, use your brain. When you have a puppy, tie a string around his neck and lead him along home."

The next day she said, "Epamanatus, go to the store for me and get me a loaf of bread." Epamanatus remembered what his mother had told him. He tied a string around the bread and dragged it home. When his mother saw the dirty, beat-up loaf of bread, she said, "Epamanatus, use your brain. When you get bread, put it under your big high hat and pull your hat on tight and run along home."

The next day she said, "Epamanatus, go to the store and get me a pound of butter." Epamanatus remembered what his mother had told him. He put the butter on his head and put his hat on over it and ran home. The sun was hot that day, and the butter melted and ran down his face and inside his shirt. When his mother saw him she said, "Epamanatus, use your brain. When you have butter, take it down to the stream and dunk it in the water and dunk it in the water and dunk it in the water until it is most cold; then wrap it up in bog leaves and bring it home."

The next day Epamanatus's mother said, "Epamanatus, your puppy has run over to your grandma's. Run along and get him." Epamanatus remembered what his mother had told him. When he got the puppy, he took it down to the stream and he dunked it in the water and he dunked it in the water and dunked it in the water until it was most cold and almost dead. Then he wrapped it up in leaves and ran along home. What do you think his mother said when she saw him?

V. Reading List

Craig, J. *Boxes.* New York: W. W. Norton & Co., 1964.

_____. *The Dragon in the Clock Box.* New York: Grosset & Dunlap, 1962.

DeRegniers, B. *The Giant Story.* New York: Harper & Brothers, 1953.

Freeman, D. *The Paper Party.* New York: Viking Press, 1974.

Gag, W. *Nothing At All.* New York: Coward, McCann, 1941.

Klimowicz, B. *Fred, Fred, Use Your Head.* New York: Abington, 1966.

Koch, D. *When the Cows Got Out.* New York: Holiday House, 1958.

Lionni, L. *Frederick.* Toronto: Pantheon Books, 1967.

McGovern, A. *Stone Soup.* New York: Scholastic Book Services, 1972.

Merrill, J., and Salbert, R. *The Very Nice Things.* New York: Harper & Brothers, 1959.

Moncure, J. *A Beach in My Bedroom.* Chicago: Child's World, 1978.

_____. *Rhyme Me a Rhyme.* Chicago: Children's Press, 1977.

_____. *The Four Magic Boxes.* Chicago: Child's World, 1978.

Sendak, M. *Where the Wild Things Are.* New York: Harper & Row Publishers, 1963.

Slobodkin, E. *Caps for Sale.* New York: William R. Scott, 1947.

Young, M. *The Imaginary Friend.* Chicago: Children's Press, 1977.

VI. Postscript

Mr. Nobody is our imaginary friend who visits the Joy School frequently during this unit. Each child has his own idea of Mr. Nobody's looks and actions. They all share their toys with him, ask him to sit by them, give him a drink of their juice. One day Amy, age four, announced that she had invited him to go home with her over the weekend. She helped him with his coat and boots and held his hand as she went out to the car. The next Monday she shared with us in some detail all the fun (and even one argument) she and Mr. Nobody had had at her house.

After this unit the children's drawings, paintings, and clay modeling activities became much more creative. They weren't trying to copy each other so much.

Teaching
the Joy
of Order,
Priorities,
and Goal Striving

9

☐ *A child who can set and accomplish a simple goal will become an adult who knows the joy of changing the world. "Let this education begin early. Teach little children the principles of order; the little girl to put the broom in its right place, to arrange the stove furniture in the neatest possible way, and everything in its own place. Teach them to lay away their clothing neatly, and where it can be found."* (Discourses of Brigham Young, *p. 211.*)

I. Examples and Description

A. *Adult:* A fireside speaker impressed me once with an uncommon answer to a common question. The question posed to him was: "With all you have to do, how do you look so relaxed?" (The boy who asked the question went on, partly for humor, partly for impact, to say that his father didn't have near as much responsibility, yet looked always frazzled and tired.) The answer was: "Each Sunday I spend some time alone, setting goals for the week—for the month on fast Sunday. I follow the priorities of family first, Church second, world third. I set objectives in each area, and if time is too short to do all I want to do, I put my goals into priority order, so that I know the most important ones will get done. Then I plan *how,* and write my plans into my weekly calendar book."

Most anxiety comes from wondering where we should be or what we ought to be doing. Most joy comes from knowing both.

The goal-striving process sparks joy in flames of changing heat and color. First comes the anticipating, "fire-laying" joy of goal setting and planning. Next comes the growing, fulfilling, "fire-igniting" joy of hard work toward the goal. Then follows the bright, confidence-renewing, "full-fire" joy of goal-reaching, and later on, the reflective, warm embers of remembering the achievement.

Children can feel each phase of the joy. The danger is that some parents, wanting high achievers, push their children to meet their (the parents') goals and end up with rebellion and negative views on accomplishment, or children who are high achievers for the wrong reasons.

Other parents, who bring about situations in which children feel for themselves the joy of setting and reaching simple goals, end up with children who find and enjoy real success.

B. *Child:* One of my clearest childhood memories is of my ninth summer, when my dad and my little brother and I built our log cabin. I remember sights: the slow-motion fall of fir trees, the wet, white notches in the logs. I remember sounds: my father's "timburrr," the ring of hammer on nail. But most of all, I remember feelings: the good tired feeling of satisfied, accomplished exhaustion at the end of the day, and the buoyant joy of standing that autumn, with my brother and my dad, and looking up at a finished cabin, an accomplished goal, a work of our own hands. We had set that goal, we two small boys and our father, a year before. We had drawn plans and figured where to get the logs, and Dad had told us it would be work—hard work. That experience taught the joy of having a goal, of working hard on that goal, of gradually seeing results, and of finishing and reaching the goal.

Our four-year-old came home from Sunday School one day and said, "My teacher asked if I thought I could learn these lines to take part in next week's lesson, and I said I could."

"Well, honey, it's a pretty long part. It will be hard, but I think you can too. How can we do it?"

"You help me."

"Okay. Look at this calendar. Here is next Sunday. How many days do we have?"

"One, two, three, four, five, six."

"And how many lines on your part?"

"One, two, three, four, five, six. Hey, we can learn one line each day."

I noticed the sparkle in her eye. She had set a progressive goal; she was pleased and proud. That night we learned the first line. It wasn't easy, but her unmodest, wide smile after she finished it was pure joy.

On the second night, as we worked on the second line,

she looked up and said, "Whew, Dad, this is hard, but I'll get it." (A miniature version of the joy of discipline, of work, of gradual, earned progress.) By Sunday, she knew the part. She delivered it with confidence and with the joy of a goal accomplished. Her Sunday School teacher has a problem now. Saren volunteers for everything, and she often says to me, "Dad, remember when we learned that part? Wasn't that fun?"

II. Methods

The joy of goal striving and achievement is like a diamond with many facets, each one a separate and distinct joy. There is the joy of knowing our long range purpose, the joy of responsibility, the joy of discipline, the joy of hard work, the joy of planning, the joy of shorter-range goals, the joy of causes and commitment, the joy of organization and order, even the joy of failing occasionally and of sometimes making mistakes.

A. *Knowing the lifetime goals.* Children are capable of understanding that the purpose and objective of mortal life is to return to the presence of God. They can also understand that the prerequisites to this are obedience, service, and family unity. A child who knows these long-range goals will become an adult who sets the right short-range goals, who has the proper priorities, who "climbs the right mountain." Teach this commitment directly by telling children who they are, where they came from, why they are here, and where they are going. (Use the story at the end of chapter 3 as a tool.)

B. *Understanding the concept of goals.* A three- or four-year old is capable of understanding the concept and nature of goals. Explain that a goal is "something good that we want and that we work for." Read the story "Jason and the Circus Money" at the end of this chapter. Ask and teach: What was Jason's goal? (To get enough money to buy a two-wheeled bike.) What was his plan to reach his goal? (To grow and sell tomatoes.) How did he do it? (With hard work.)

C. *Experiencing a goal.* A three- or four-year-old can experience the joy of setting and achieving a simple goal. Ask the child if he can think of a goal for himself. Help him decide on one. It might be self-improvement: learning to zip his coat, flush the toilet, or walk across the street safely. It might be solving a problem: not getting so dirty at school, or not sucking his thumb anymore. It might be making a new friend, or earning money to buy something special.

Write the goal down and put a big circle by it. Periodically, as the goal is achieved, let the child fill in part of the circle. (When the goal is half-completed, the circle will be half filled in.)

Help the child develop a plan to meet his goal, such as asking the neighbors if they need work done, trying to zip his coat each night before he goes to bed, not kneeling down in the dirt, inviting a new child over to play, or putting his blanket away (the one he holds while sucking his thumb).

Praise the setting of the goal, praise the plan, praise every step the child takes toward the goal. Always relate your praise (or your criticism) to *what he has done,* and not to him. Instead of calling a child a good boy or a bad boy, call the thing he's done a good thing or a bad thing. Thus you reestablish your love for him as unconditional, as something that does not fluctuate with his goods or bads.

D. *Feeling the joy of setting goals and working together.* Have family goals planned and set together. These might be anything worthwhile, from reading the Book of Mormon to doing the spring housecleaning together as a family. Involve the children. Write down the goal and plan it first together; go to work on it; then discuss the results of each phase—how you are doing, how it makes you feel as each part is achieved.

Do the kinds of chores together in which results are visible, such as pulling weeds, washing windows, raking leaves, or waxing the floor or car. Part of the joy comes from seeing the result.

Reflect together on achievements after the fact: "Wasn't it great!" "Doesn't it look fine now that it is done!" "Isn't it nice to rest after getting it all finished!"

Have family jobs and responsibilities for each family member. For example, a little child can be in charge of clearing off the dishes after Sunday dinner. Again, lavish praise on the child, saying, "Doesn't that look nice?" Make a chart showing each family member's responsibility, and discuss these responsibilities in family home evening.

Family responsibilities can often be given to a child that relate to that particular child's gifts. Saren, whose personality has a particularly calming effect on the other children, has been designated our "family peacemaker." Shawni, with her passion for having things in place, is our "family orderkeeper." Josh (mostly due to wishful thinking by his parents) is our "obedience policeman." And happy little Saydi is our "family joygiver." It is amazing how each one takes his responsibility, reminds the others, and, most of all, becomes better at his assignment himself.

As you work together, teach by example the joy of discipline, of working hard and getting it done, and of afterwards feeling the fulfillment.

E. *Games and stories that illustrate and teach the joy of achieving.*

*1. Play games with timers. Can they do it before the buzzer?

*2. Tell stories that illustrate the joy of doing a good job and taking pride, such as "The Three Little Pigs."

F. *Teach the law of the harvest.* The joy of goal achievement and the law of the harvest are "Siamese twins"—they are inseparable. There is security in knowing you will reap what you plant. Teach this joy by actually sowing and actually reaping.

One way is to have a garden. Let the children plant, weed, water, and harvest. Then use the example of the garden as a way to explain many things: how brushing the teeth grows up into the joy of no cavities, how kind deeds grow up into the joy of happy feelings, how selfish deeds grow up like weeds to choke the family.

Another way is to teach children to save. We have a family bank that consists of a box with a lock on it. Each child has a bank book, kept in a special drawer for safety so it won't be lost. In the bank book, the banker (Daddy) records and initials all deposits or withdrawals and pays interest at the end of each month. Children learn number skills, but more importantly, they learn the joy and satisfaction that come from saving and seeing money grow.

G. *Organization and order.* Have a good set of shelves in a child's room. Help him organize his possessions, with a place for each item. Then give strong encouragement and praise as he keeps things in their places. The simple lessons of order in a child's life will go a long way in building the critical, later-life skill of organizing his thoughts and ideas.

Teach a child to put one toy away before taking the next toy out. Explain that this way he will know where his things are and will not have to play in a cluttered room.

"The Gunny Bag": Get a large bag (such as an old mail sack or a big plastic bag) that "lives" in some out-of-the-way place like the basement or the attic. Paint or draw a face on it and introduce it to the children as "The Gunny Bag" who comes around when we least expect and "eats up" all toys that are left out. He then returns to his cave. On Saturday he comes and coughs them up, but if he eats the same thing twice he may never give it back. He cries and cries when he can't find anything to eat.

Children will love making the "Gunny Bag" cry, and will be more aware, since he can come at any moment, of keeping things orderly and putting one thing away before taking something else out.

H. *The joy of mistakes and failure.* Discuss your own failures. Show your children that you are not perfect, but that you accept your failings and try to learn from them. The key here is simple: praise them as much when they fail as when they succeed. Praise the try, not the result. Praise the effort and show how it might be tried again more successfully. Always encourage trial and error. Set the example by being both a good loser and a good winner. And finally, tell and show how some goals take a great deal of time and effort before they can be achieved.

I. *Share some of your goals with your children.* The fact that you are reading this book probably indicates that you have a goal of being a better parent. Why not share that goal with your children? Tell them that your goal is to be the best daddy or mommy, and that you need their help on your goal, that you want them to tell you how you can improve. (It's an interesting experience to have a four-year-old tell you you've got to stop getting mad at the lawn mower.) This process of asking will teach children, by example, that it is good to seek others' help, that asking for help is not weakness, but intelligence. Then, later on, *they* will ask *you.*

III. Family Focal Point: Sunday Goal-Setting Sessions

I have the habit of isolating one hour each Sunday to set goals and make plans for the week ahead. One week, four-year-old Saren interrupted: "What are you doing in here, Daddy?" I contained the "go back out and play" instinct and told her I was setting goals. "What are goals?" I simplified: "Things you want to try really hard to do." "Can I have a goal?" "Sure. What do you want to try hard to do?" "Skip rope." "Okay, Saren. You sit here and draw a picture of yourself skipping rope. That will show your goal." It was the beginning of a tradition at our house. Every Sunday now, just before church, each family member over three either draws or writes his goal, putting a circle by it to color in when he meets the goal. We call this our "Sunday session." Then, the next night in family home evening, we take a moment to discuss the goals, to praise, to encourage, and to talk about how past goals have been met. A child's Sunday session time can also be an opportunity to think about the week ahead and to help him understand a calendar so he can look forward to events of the week and plan which days he will work on his goal. It is also a time when I can have a brief "interview" with each child as he tells me his goals and as I focus on him individually and make him feel important through my interest and my praise. The children have taken to using this weekly interview as a time to tell me of the private problems or worries they have.

IV. Story: "Jason and the Circus Money"

It was Saturday morning and Jason was watching television. Between two shows there was a commercial about the circus. On the screen were elephants and dancing bears and clowns. A voice said, "The circus will be in your town in two weeks! Don't miss it!"

Jason ran to tell his mother he couldn't miss the circus. His mother said, "Jason, we've just spent a lot of money on your birthday. If you want to go to that circus, you'll have to earn enough money to buy your own ticket."

Jason thought hard about that—so hard that he didn't even watch the rest of the TV show. He looked under all the cushions on the couch and chairs and found two dimes. He went and asked his mother how much a ticket cost. She said, "Two dollars." "How many dimes is that?" asked Jason. "Twenty," said his mother. "As many as all of your fingers and all your toes." "I've got two already," Jason said, holding up his dimes. His mother smiled at him and took his hand. "Come with me," she said.

Jason's mother got a large sheet of paper and drew a big, king-size "20" on it. Then she made a long tube by the side with some marks on it. The paper looked like this:

She colored in two squares in the tube with a red
crayon, like this:

Jason got the idea before she even told him. He said,
"Every time I get another dime, I'll color a square until I
get up to 20!" "Right," said his mother, "and there are
some old soda bottles in the basement that are worth ten
cents each."

Jason found three bottles in the basement. He put them
in his red wagon and pulled them around the corner to the
grocery store. He got three dimes and colored in three more
squares.

"What now, Mom?" Jason said. "Well, I don't know,"
said his mother. "Can you think of any more ways to earn
some more dimes?" Jason said, "More pop bottles." His
mother said, "Sorry, that's all we've got." Jason said,
"Maybe Mr. Johnson next door has some. I'll go see." Mr.
Johnson didn't have any old pop bottles, but he did have a
backyard that needed cleaning, and he told Jason he
would give him two dimes to do it. Jason did it.

Jason kept thinking of things. By Saturday, do you
know what his chart looked like? That's right, it was completely filled in—and it was a very good circus!

On the way home from the circus, Jason was thinking
very hard. He said, "Mom, do you think I could ever earn
enough money to buy myself a two-wheeled bike?" "I
think so," said his mother, "but it would take a long time."

That night his parents had a long talk—and got a good
idea. The next morning Jason's father said, "Jason, I think
if you were to raise some tomatoes in the garden this year,
you could earn enough to buy a bike. Let's use two dollars
of my money to buy some tomato plants. If you take good
care of them and sell the tomatoes when they grow, you
can get enough money to give me back my two dollars and
to buy your very own bike."

All summer Jason watered his plants and pulled the weeds out. When the tomatoes got red, he picked them and put them in a bucket; then he knocked on the neighbor's doors. "Would you like to buy some tomatoes?" he said. "Only a nickel each." Every day more tomatoes were red. Every day Jason sold them. By autumn Jason had sold all the tomatoes. He had enough money to pay his father the two dollars and also to buy one present for himself: a red bike, the same color as those tomatoes.

V. Reading List

Burton, V. L. *Mike Mulligan and His Steam Shovel.* Boston: Houghton Mifflin Co., 1939.

Conaway, J. *Will I Ever Be Good Enough?* Milwaukee: Raintree Publishers, 1977.

Felt, S. *Rosa Too Little.* New York: Doubleday & Co., 1950.

Greene, C. *I Want to Be a Baseball Player.* Chicago: Children's Press, 1963.

Holl, A. *George the Gentle Giant.* New York: Golden Press, 1962.

Keats, E. J. *Whistle for Willie.* New York: Scholastic Book Services, 1964.

Lexan, J. M. *Benjie.* New York: The Dial Press, 1964.

Moncure, J. *All by Myself.* Chicago: Child's World, 1976.

_____. *See My Garden Grow.* Chicago: Child's World, 1977.

Riley, S. *What Does It Mean? Success.* Chicago: Child's World, 1978.

Taylor, Barbara J. *I Can Do.* Provo, Utah: Brigham Young University Press, 1972.

VI. Postscript

A. Dannie, age four, had set a goal at Joy School to sit still and be quiet when it was the teacher's turn to talk. She was a very active child, and it was difficult for her to pay attention. As she sat, with arms folded and a serious expression on her face, another child leaned over and said something to her. "Don't bother me," said Dannie, "I'm working on my goal."

B. Cathy, age four and a half, had reached the goal she was working on at school—zipping up her coat—and had chosen another goal to work on at home. Her mother reported that she brought her "special blanket" and said, "Put this on top of the refrigerator where I can't reach it. My new goal is to stop sucking my thumb." It wasn't easy, especially at night, but with the help and encouragement of her parents, Cathy broke her thumb-sucking habit within two or three weeks. She was very proud of herself, and brought her chart, which she had made herself and posted on her refrigerator, with the circle all colored in to share with the children at school.

EMOTIONAL JOYS

"Homes are made permanent through love. Though you neglect some of your business, though you neglect some of your cattle, though you fail to produce full crops, study to hold your children's love." (David O. McKay, Stepping Stones, *p. 298.*)

"I believe in indulging children, in a reasonable way. If the little girls want dolls, shall they have them? Yes. But must they be taken to the dressmakers to be dressed? No. Let the girls learn to cut and sew the clothing for their dolls, and in a few years they will know how to make a dress for themselves and others. Let the little boys have tools, and let them make their sleds, little wagons, etc., and when they grow up, they are acquainted with the use of tools and can build a carriage, a house, or anything else." (Discourses of Brigham Young, *p. 210.*)

"All happy families resemble one another. Each unhappy family is unhappy in its own way." (Leo Tolstoy.)

Preserving the Joy of Trust and the Basic Confidence to Try

10

☐ *"The first thing that is taught by the mother to the child should be true; we should never allow ourselves to teach our children one thing and practice another. . . . [Parents] should never teach them anything unless they know it is correct in every respect."* (Discourses of Brigham Young, *pp. 206-7.*)

I. *Examples and Description*

A. *Child:* Our two-year-old Shawni came along to her older sister's dancing class. We were watching the older sister, and left the two-year-old sitting down the row of seats. I glanced over and saw her eyes growing wider. The next moment she was up, twirling, whirling, a two-year-old facsimile of modern dance. She wanted to try, to experience.

It was November, and when we got home after the dancing class it was still light and the first snow of the year was falling. Little Shawni happened to be the last one out of the car. She lagged behind in the driveway, and when I went back after her, she was sitting Indian-style in a drift, rubbing snow into her hair. Snow was new to her, and she was experiencing it in the most intimate way she could think of.

This is a joy to preserve, a joy that small children almost always have but they often lose early. (Think of the three-year-old afraid to touch the snow or the four-year-old too shy to sit on Santa's knee.) The symptoms of the loss of this joy are the phrases we have all heard: "Oh, I can't do it." "Will you help me? I'm afraid."

When did they lose it? Where do they leave it? Why? It is our fault. We fail to preserve it in three ways. First, in our preoccupations and "busyness," we fail ourselves to experience new things and to manifest the joy that comes from them. Failure no. 1: lack of example.

Second, again in our involvement with "more important things," we fail to praise and encourage their exploration. The encouragement could be verbal or, better yet, could be expressed by us learning from them, trying things with them. By criticizing instead of praising, we build fear and rub out the continuing desire to try. A child performs an important experiment by pouring his milk into his soup, and we call him a mess. A child takes off his shoes to see how the grass feels, and we tell him "that's silly," and doesn't he know he will get dirty. A child pats a big, friendly dog on the head, and we say, "Watch out, he might bite you." A child picks a flower to give to a friend, and we tell her she didn't get enough of the stem to fit in the vase. Failure no. 2: criticism instead of praise.

Third, we often compare our children with each other or with other children, thus making them feel inferior. Johnny tries to run a race or improve on the piano and glows with the joy of trying until we say, "Say, that Jones boy sure is learning fast," or "I wonder how the Smith girl got so good on the piano? She's only had lessons for as long as Johnny." A four-year-old wants to climb the monkey bars, or go up a little ladder at the shallow end of the pool, or climb up on the shed in the backyard, and we say, "No, no, you'll fall and get hurt. Don't try it by yourself." Failure no. 3: discouragement by comparison or by over-done caution.

Again we've got it backwards. It's children who have the joy of spontaneity, of trying new things, of trusting. We should be learning, not teaching. We should be following and encouraging their lead, not leading with our own lost ability. If we do, the joy of trust and trying can come back into our adult lives.

B. *Adult:* I spent a summer in Hawaii one year working and saving money for the next year of school. I had a friend there named Kathy. It was the first week in Hawaii for both of us. We had just met each other, and we had both just met a Hawaiian named Kiki. Kiki invited us to a beach party, "a real Hawaiian one," he said. It was on a Saturday afternoon, on a beach at the far side of the island.

As I recall, the party had three distinct parts: surfing, eating, and dancing. My inclination was to watch all three. Her inclination was to do all three.

I can remember her out in the surf, trying to catch a wave, missing one, getting tipped over by the next, falling off the board until she was exhausted. What I remember is her face. Kathy was not an exceptionally pretty girl, but in that surf her face was radiant, her eyes dancing with the joy of trying something new, of feeling a new sensation. She was not embarrassed or self-conscious because she couldn't do it yet. She felt—and her face showed it—a simple childlike joy of the moment.

Finally dark came and the huge beach bonfire was lit. It was time to eat. I had never seen poi and neither had Kathy. My instinct was to bury it while no one was looking; her instinct was to eat it and love it. I watched her expression, the corners of her mouth, for signs of distaste or of the discomfort of something foreign. Instead I saw delight—not that she had an immediate taste for poi (no one does), but she loved the experience, the new texture, the opportunity to know how it did taste. She added a little sugar and ate the whole bowlful.

Then came the dancing. There was an extra grass skirt. Right away Kathy was trying her first hula. Compared to the swaying perfection of the brown-skinned Hawaiians, Kathy was clumsy, but there was no inhibition in her clumsiness, no discomfort or embarrassment. Her smile, her sparkle, her obvious enjoyment of the moment compensated, and somehow she looked almost good at it.

The very purpose of life is experience, and the joy of trying things and of new participation and new interest is a classic and significant joy. There is so much to do in the world, so many good things to try, 360 degrees of experience. Most of us eat the same narrow 10-degree sliver of the pie over and over again, too afraid or inhibited (or sophisticated?) to try the other 350 degrees. Somewhere we have lost our grasp of the joy of the basic confidence to try.

The telltale symptoms of children who are losing this joy are their words: "Oh, I'm no good at that." "You help me do it. I can't by myself." "I don't want to try it, I've never done it before." Now we "turncoat" on them; we push them; we say, "Don't be so shy—don't be so scared—you won't get hurt—come on, at least try."

First we create the fear, the hesitancy; then we criticize it, which, of course, magnifies it and makes it worse.

There are two kinds of basic fears in the world: fear of getting hurt and fear of failure. Both are tools of the adversary: both work against God's purposes and objectives for us. "For God hath not given us the spirit of fear; but of power, and of love, and of a sound mind." (2 Timothy 1:7.) Both kinds of fear apply to all facets of life. We fear failure mentally, spiritually, physically, emotionally, and socially, and we fear being hurt physically, emotionally, and socially. Both fears are self-fulfilling. Physical fear often causes physical hurt, and fear of failing almost always causes failure.

Children are born with neither of these two fears; it is the learning of the fears that takes away the joy. Perhaps the easiest way to look at preserving the joy of trust and the basic confidence to try is to look at its synonym, "avoiding the conveyance of the fear of being hurt and the fear of failure." Remember, this is a "preserving" chapter; the parents' challenge is not to teach children, but to avoid destroying what they already have.

II. Methods

A. Understand the delicacy of a child's confidence, of his desire to try. In her book *Times to Remember*, Rose Kennedy speaks of the physical freedom she gave her children at Hyannis Port, Massachusetts. They could climb, explore, try new things. There were skinned knees and even broken arms—but her book correctly relates physical freedom to physical confidence, and physical confidence to every other kind of confidence (and regardless of their overall opinion of the Kennedy family, most people would agree that they did and do possess great confidence). The point is that a broken arm is better than a broken spirit. Of course, a healthy respect for real danger is important, but that is different from the overcautious fear of physical hurt that many children develop.

B. *Let children try things physically.* Break down and try things with them. Climb a tree. Jump off the diving board. It will do you good and give verbal and nonverbal encouragement to your children's physical confidence. Particularly, try things you are not good at. Let the children see that lack of skill is no reason for not trying. Lack of physical fear promotes coordination. When you think of it, athletic coordination and ability are, in large part, an absence of physical fear and inhibition.

The trick is to create a basically safe environment, rather than having to constantly warn about physical danger. Fence the creek until the children are old enough to wade in it; put the porcelain figurines up high until they are old enough not to break them.

C. *Win and keep the children's trust.* The quality we call trust is basically an absence of the fear of being hurt— physically or emotionally or socially. The child who "jumps to daddy" trusts that he won't be dropped. The child who is nice to his friend trusts his friend to be nice to him. The child who returns your love trusts your love for him.

Children trust us until we violate their trust. A broken trust not only hurts them at the moment, but it also hurts permanently because it teaches fear of being hurt. Keep their trust by never lying, even a little. Don't say, "The doctor won't hurt you." Don't say you'll spank them if they do it again and then not spank them when they do. Don't tell them to tell the telephone caller you're not at home. Don't forget a promise. If they never learn to doubt you on small things, then they'll never doubt your compliments to them, your advice to them, your love for them.

D. *Don't snap-judge your children.* Don't condemn them without a trial, without knowledge of the facts and circumstances. We assume an arrested man is innocent until proven guilty, but often we fail to give our children the same benefit of the doubt.

E. *Encourage children to try new things.* Look for and set up new experiences. When they ask for help, first say, "I'll be here to help, but try it first." Then praise the try as much as or more than the success.

F. *Understand the need for encouragement.* It has been said that when we can see failure as an indispensable way of learning, we free the mind and the spirit. What a lesson! When the basic confidence to try is replaced with the fear of failure, a child's outgoing joy is replaced with in-turning doubt. Children, like fragile flowers, can be crushed so easily by the fingers of criticism and comparative judgment; bright, innovative attempts can be replaced with sullen fear to try.

Parents hold the control lever. Parental encouragement will win out over "other-people" discouragement. A "Good try!" from parents can counterbalance scoffs from peers. It is so important to try to avoid saying no unless real danger is involved. Instead, try saying "Let's try it a different way," or "Wouldn't this be better?" Substitute the positive for the negative.

G. *Praise the attempt.* To praise the result when the result is not good violates the trust. But to praise the try, to compliment the effort—this sort of praise will bring about more tries and eventually more success. We thus teach that there is such a thing as successful failure: failure from which we learn and grow. "It's okay not to be able to do it. It's okay to miss, to fall down, to make a mistake. This is how we grow."

By not teaching the fear of being hurt or the fear of failure, we can help preserve children's joy of trust and the basic confidence to try. However, the two greatest keys in the safeguarding process are the two related joys that children do not inherently possess. These two joys follow in the next two chapters: "The Joy of Confidence in Self as a Unique Individual" and "The Joy of Security and Identity as Part of a Unified Family." Family security and unique individual confidence can preserve forever the joy of trust and the basic confidence to try, and can even restore the trust and confidence that some children have already lost.

III. Family Focal Point: Daddy Dates and Mommy Dates

Our four-year-old Shawni doesn't know the days of the week by name—she knows them by activity: "Church Day," "Family Home Evening Day," "Daddy Doesn't Go to Work Day." Wednesday is "Daddy Date Day." We take half an hour after work when she is in charge, and we listen. We go where she wants, talk about what she thinks of. I encourage her as she tries things, as she says and thinks things. I reinforce her basic confidence. I watch for teaching moments that can give her the understanding that eliminates fear. Most of all, I am alone with her, learning from her the joy of trust and the basic confidence to try. What I learn from her I mirror back to her so she'll know that it is good.

IV. Story: "Pedro the Squirrel"

A whole town of squirrels lived in the trees at the top of the hill. It was a perfect place to live, with hollow trunks for houses, lively branches and boughs for running and leaping, and plenty of sunshine. And it was far enough up the mountain that the wolves didn't come past very often. The only problem was that the nut trees were quite far away. But never mind, all the men and boy squirrels ran every day in the autumn to the nut trees and filled up a big box with nuts. Then they dragged the box back to the trees at the top of the hill to be stored for winter.

All the boy squirrels except Pedro helped out. Pedro was the smallest squirrel, and his legs were too short to go all the way. He tried it once, but he couldn't pull hard enough to help very much. "Never you mind," his father would say. "Some squirrels are fast and have long legs, and others are strong. Each one is good at something. You are good at thinking of new ideas."

It was true. Pedro did have lots of ideas. He thought he would be an inventor when he grew up. But most of his friends thought it was better to be strong and to run fast than to be an inventor.

One day Pedro was thinking of new ideas, and he thought of the idea of putting wheels on the big box. Late that night he made two wheels and put them on the nut box. Sure enough, it was much easier to pull than before when it didn't have the wheels. In fact, Pedro could pull it all by himself. Pedro was excited, but he was so tired from thinking of the wheels that he fell asleep in the box.

The next morning all the strong squirrels grabbed the ropes to drag the box to the nut tree. (They didn't even see little Pedro asleep in the box.) Hey, how easily the box pulled along! Were they stronger? No—it was those round things on the bottom. Who put them there? What were they? All the excitement woke up Pedro. He popped up from the box and told the other squirrels about the wheels.

What a hero Pedro became! With the wheels, the squirrels could make six trips a day to the nut tree instead of just one. After that day, Pedro was never afraid to say anything and never afraid to try out any of his new ideas.

V. Reading List

Anderson, C. *Crooked Colt.* New York: The Macmillan Co., 1954.

Conaway, J. *Will I Ever Be Good Enough?* Milwaukee: Raintree Publishers, 1977.

Friskey, M. *Seven Diving Ducks.* Milwaukee: E.M. Hale & Co., 1965.

Kraus, R. *The Trouble with Spiders.* New York: Harper & Row Publishers, 1962.

Moncure, J. *All By Myself.* Chicago: The Child's World, 1977.

Piper, W. *The Little Engine that Could.* New York: Platt & Munk Co., 1954.

Seuss, Dr. *Green Eggs and Ham.* New York: Beginners Books, 1960.

Tobias, T. *Easy or Hard?* Chicago: Children's Press, 1977.

Williams, G. *Timid Timothy.* New York: William R. Scott, 1944.

Zolotow, C. *Over and Over.* New York: Harper & Brothers, 1957.

VI. *Postscript*

A. One day the children had made their own sandwiches in school for a little picnic. Doug, age three, an only child who was used to being waited on, surprised his mother that evening by saying, "I can spread my own bread." The bread was soft and the butter was hard, but Doug did his best. When the bread broke into several pieces, Doug said, "That's okay. Everyone makes mistakes sometimes. I'll probably do better next time."

B. Several children were playing a beanbag toss game, but Brant said, "I don't know how." The teacher talked him into trying, and each time he tossed the beanbag, the other children said, "Nice try, Brant." He relaxed a little, and even though he never threw the beanbag through the hole, he was laughing and enjoying the game.

Teaching
the Joy
of Family
Security,
Identity,
and Pride

11

☐ *"A child has the right to feel that in his home he has a place of refuge, a place of protection from the dangers and evils of the outside world." (David O. McKay,* Stepping Stones, *p. 323.)*

> *"To make a happy fireside clime*
> *To weans and wife,*
> *That's the true pathos and sublime*
> *O' human life." (Robert Burns.)*

I. Examples and Description

A. *Adult:* When I was growing up, I knew a group of brothers and sisters, schoolmates of mine. I was always impressed because they seemed so unconcerned about being with the "in group" or the "right people." They didn't even care much about wearing the newest thing, the latest style. They were all friendly, though, and all well liked. They seemed so secure, unafraid of failure.

Each of the six had his own personality, but all possessed one similar quality, a quality that I grew to greatly admire. It was a peace, a calm, a security, a naturalness, a confidence. None of these adjectives quite describe it, but it was there. You could feel it; you knew they had it. I was always interested in where it came from. It wasn't from individual brilliance, or from exceptional athletic abilities, or from particular handsomeness or beauty; they were pretty average in each of these categories. The clue seemed to be in their love and acceptance of each other.

I remember that one boy played on the high school basketball team. He sat on the bench most of the time, but I noticed that his brothers and sisters were always at the games, all of them—and I knew a couple of them well enough to know that they had little interest in basketball. They supported each other. Each had his own circle of friends, but none were ever too busy with friends to have time for a brother or sister.

One day an unexpected opportunity came to discover the true source of their confidence. The family moved into a house just through the block from my house. Now, instead of seeing them just in school, I saw them at home, and the secret was revealed! The confidence, the assurance, the security, the unity came from the unconditional love of their home. From the outside their home was ordinary; on the inside it was extraordinary.

I remember the youngest child, who was just turning two. The first words he ever said were "Ah, mush," a phrase often used in the family in mock-fun-poking at the frequent hugs and pats and physical affection that were shown in the home.

I was with one of the sons one day as he brought home a not-so-good school grade, a grade he hated to show his father. I wish I could describe the father's reaction. There was no anger, no belittling, no criticism, just a look that somehow said, "Son, a grade could never alter my love and respect for you; I have complete confidence in you. I just assume there is a reason for this grade, and you don't need to tell me what it is." I remember suddenly realizing that my friend's apprehension about showing the grade was not because of fear that his father would be critical or angry, but because he knew his father *wouldn't* be angry. He knew his father loved him unconditionally, and he was proud of him unconditionally.

But at the same time my friend was proud to be a part of a strong family, a family that had a tradition of doing its best, and he felt bad that he had let down that tradition and that family with the poor grade. He was motivated by love, not fear; by a desire to please and be part of his great family, rather than by apprehension of criticism or of anger.

Yes, I know now that the secret was the warmth and acceptance and security of that home—a joy irreplaceable, and unavailable from any other source.

B. *Child:* I'll always remember our daughter's prayer on the evening before Linda and I left on a week's vacation. Saren was four and was looking forward to spending the week with her grandmother. Still, she knew our family would be separated for a time, and she felt concern. She said, "Please bless us while our family will be halfed."

She felt the security of family and missed that security when we weren't together. I also remember the joy in her face the night we got back together and knelt again in family prayer. I saw her smile contentedly as we all held hands in the circle. She said, "Thanks that our family is back together and happy again."

Benjamin Franklin thought so much of the goodness and naturalness of marriage that he likened a single person to half a pair of scissors. Something similar, perhaps even stronger, could be said about a child without a loving, unified family. No child of any age has enough confidence or emotional independence to successfully exist as an island, untied, with nothing to cling to or be one with.

A family can be a base, a bastion of unconditional love that a child can always turn to after failure, after a disappointment, after being hurt or rebuffed or intimidated. There he can return to love, to a unit that he will always be part of, always welcome in, always important in.

I once asked a group of young people what they thought heaven might be like, how they imagined it. As they described their impressions, their words seemed to focus on two key elements: who will and won't be there, and what will and won't be happening there.

Think about those two factors for a minute. *Who will and won't be there?* Will: people you love, who love you. Won't: people who hurt you, use you, embarrass you. *What will and won't happen there?* Will: progress, growth, beauty, happy new experience. Won't: fear, failure, ridicule.

Suddenly a new meaning for an old phrase came alive in my mind: "The home can be a heaven on earth." Why not? Do we not control both who is in our home and what happens there? Cannot the home, therefore, be a place of sanctuary, of security, of sharing, of progress, of love—in short, a heaven?

Virtually all concerned parents in the Church have participated at one time or another in the classic debate of "Where is the ideal place to raise children? In Utah or out of Utah? In the city or country? Small towns or large towns?" It is an endless debate with one true answer: "None of the above." Children are not reared in the city or the country, in Zion or in the mission field, they are reared in the home. If the home means a unified family, an environment of unconditional love, then other environmental elements by comparison are of little consequence.

II. Methods

A. "Family Institution." Security and confidence are bred from membership in institutions. A great university, a great fraternity, a great corporation—each lends strength and well-being to its members. Institutions surround people with a mother-henlike emotional protection, giving them an identity, a pride, a thing to be a part of.

Institutions become institutions by virtue of traditions, accepted norms that become part of the institution, part of the identity. For example, a school has school songs, a school symbol, a school mascot, school codes, school decisions, school councils, school trips, school games, and school jokes. Now take the "school" off each and add "family," and you have a family institution.

B. Genealogy. Children love knowing "where they came from" in the genealogical sense. Some ways to convey this:

First, frame old family pictures and group them together on a special wall.

Second, tell true stories about the parents as children, including memories about grandparents. These will become the favorite bedtime stories and will get a child in touch with his roots. For one of our most successful family projects, we have taken a large, hardbound ledger book and turned it into what we call our "Ancestor Book." The two of us have written stories in children's language about our parents, grandparents, and great-grandparents—

simple incidents and experiences from their lives, particularly their childhoods. Best of all, the children have illustrated the stories and therefore seem to remember every detail. It has become the children's favorite storybook, and I sometimes feel sure that I see a distinct look of pride on their faces as they hear of the courage and good deeds of their ancestors.

Third, draw a simple family tree, with each child as a branch and the parents as the trunk. Put pictures of the parents and grandparents on the appropriate trunk and roots and of brothers and sisters on the limbs. Frame it and hang it on the same wall as the ancestor pictures.

C. *Consistency.* Children need to be able to depend on certain constants in their lives. Predictable, consistent things build security. Inconsistency breeds fear and insecurity.

There are four places where consistency is particularly important: (1) In discipline. If a family law is broken, the punishment or consequence should be automatic —expected—consistent. (2) In example. Make yourself predictable to them—always doing right in their presence, but admitting mistakes. (3) In regular schedules for certain important things such as the evening meal or the weekly family home evening. (4) In always keeping promises.

D. *Constant awareness of each other.* (1) Leave notes to each other, perhaps on the refrigerator, telling where you are and when you will be back. (2) Support each other's activities. If one participates in a school play, all attend. (3) Show love for spouse openly. As the saying goes, "The greatest thing a father can do for his children is to love their mother."

E. *Display open gratitude for children.* How simple—and how incredibly important—it is to let a child know he is wanted and needed, how precious and important he is to the family.

1. Tell the child the story at the end of chapter 3 about where he came from. Tell him the story of how his parents

wanted a child and prayed for one, and how the Lord chose him to come to this family. Tell "how much we wanted you," "how much we prayed to Heavenly Father for you," "how happy we were when you arrived with us."

*2. Make up a paper chain linked into a circle with a family member's name on every other link and the word *love* on the links between the names. Show how important each link is: if one comes out, no more chain.

F. *Working together.* We always do the evening dishes together. With six of us working at it, it only takes ten minutes—our record is seven and a half—and there is something about working together, in teamwork, that is fun. It leaves the whole load on no one and stimulates interesting conversation. Our six-year-old Shawni loves to repeat over and over, like a locomotive, while we're working: "Many hands make light work." It's true—and furthermore, many hands, working together, make a strong family.

III. *Family Focal Point: Family Traditions*

As mentioned, there is great security in belonging—to a club, a fraternity, an association, an institution, an entity with which one can identify. Children who think of their family as an institution have a powerful sense of belonging, of identity, of security. We decided years ago that we would like that identity and association to be so strong in our family that if one of our children were asked the many-option question "Who are you?" his second response (after "a child of God") would be "a member of my family."

A family should be an institution. A family should not be people grouped together for convenience, where children live until they can be on their own, any more than a great university should be a group of buildings full of books and people. Someone once defined an institution as "something with rules and traditions and pride." Certainly a family should have all three. We have talked about the first one in chapter 2. The middle one, traditions, can be the key to the third one, pride, and can provide tremendous momentary joy as well as build within children the secure feeling of being part of a great institution.

Here are a few of our family traditions, just for the sake of illustration:

1. A report on the day from each family member around the dinner table.

2. "Welcome the new season" family outings, such as a picnic at the start of summer or sleigh riding with the first snow.

3. Evening prayer in a family circle, holding hands.

4. Reading the Book of Mormon together after Sunday dinner.

5. Reserving one part of family home evening for a clear-the-air "gripe session."

6. A particular birthday cake shape for each birthday: a clown cake for all three-year-olds, an elephant for four-year-olds, and so on.

7. Sending a family picture Thanksgiving card to friends each year.

8. Particularly special Christmas traditions. For example, bake a birthday cake for Jesus, or serve a "Nazareth supper" of fish, bread, and grape juice on Christmas Eve. Family members dress as and play the roles of Mary's family on the night before she and Joseph leave for Bethlehem. At dinner discuss being careful on the journey, what the angel said about the baby, and how blessed the family is to be part of the Lord's birth.

Last year, Daddy, playing the part of Mary's father, asked eight-year-old Saren, playing Mary, "Oh, Mary, don't you think you could wait just until the baby is born before you and Joseph go to Bethlehem?" Saren answered, very lovingly but very firmly, "No, father. You know what King Herod is like, and we wouldn't want him mad at us now, would we?" Joseph, played by four-year-old Josh, chimed in, "Mary's right, Dad. We've got to leave tomorrow." After supper, we act out the nativity scene, complete with innkeepers, shepherds, wise men, and animals.

Another Christmas tradition is a nativity scene of small clay figures, with an empty manger. Each time a child does a kind deed for another member of the family, he is allowed to put one straw into the tiny manger. The more kind deeds that are done, the softer the manger will be when the figure of the baby Jesus is placed in it on Christmas Eve.

We also like to prepare a self-produced 8mm movie of family members doing day-by-day things. This, along with a child-narrated sound track on cassette tape, is sent to far-away grandparents for a special Christmas gift.

Each child buys his own Christmas gifts. The children save their pennies, and we take each one shopping individually to a variety store, where he can buy something for each family member with his own money. Each child wraps his own gifts completely by himself. These gifts are opened on the morning of December 24 so the larger "Santa gifts" don't overshadow them.

Without any question, our children feel more joy in giving and in seeing their brothers and sisters open their gifts than in receiving. One example was three-year-old Saydi running across the room, throwing her arms around Josh, and saying, "Thank you for the bee. I love it!" (Four-year-old Josh had picked a fifty-cent wind-up bee that flapped its wings.) The real joy was on Josh's face an hour later when he tugged on my sleeve and beamed up at me, saying, "Dad, Saydi loved that bee I got her, didn't she!"

During the week before Christmas, each child also chooses one toy that is still new and still loved to give to a less fortunate child. As a group, the family goes to an orphanage and gives the wrapped gifts. Shawni can still remember with great joy the name and virtually every detail about the little orphan girl to whom she gave her doll three years ago.

A gift for Jesus is another cherished tradition. Each family member writes on a piece of paper something that he is going to do for Jesus during the new year and puts the paper into a special box. The gifts are pulled out and read two or three times during the year at a family home evening.

Such Christmas traditions, as they are recalled and discussed during the year, can be great ongoing vehicles for teaching children joy.

9. Sometimes rather small, unpretentious things become the finest traditions. We love popcorn in our family, and it is the only thing Daddy can cook. We found a very special kind of popcorn in the store once and liked it so well that we bought several cases. When I took out a bottle one day I shook it like a rhythm rattle, and spontaneously little Saydi started to dance. The other children joined in. Now, every time we have popcorn, we have to do the "popcorn dance." It's a tradition.

IV. Story: "Fluffy Needs His Family"

Once upon a time there was a baby goose. He was so soft and downy that he was called Fluffy. He had three brothers and three sisters, and every day he had swimming lessons from his beautiful mother. He and his brothers and sisters swam in a line behind their mother. Fluffy was fourth in the line. He always had three sisters in front of him and three brothers behind him. Each evening when they swam to shore they saw their father, who was finishing an extension on the family nest.

Whenever Fluffy didn't know something, he asked his mother or father. Whenever he didn't know how to do something, they helped him. Whenever he was hungry, they caught some tasty little bugs for him to eat. Whenever he wanted to play, he played with his three brothers and three sisters. His mother made sure he was warm; his father made sure he was safe.

Fluffy learned that his last name was Honker. That was his parents' name; that was his family name. Fluffy was proud to have that name, and proud to swim behind his mother, and proud to see his father able to do so much and fly so fast.

One day a big storm came, and the wind blew so hard

that it made big waves on the pond. Mother Honker started to swim for shore and the babies followed, but it was rainy and foggy and hard to see. Suddenly Fluffy saw a big wave go up in front of him. He couldn't see his mother. He couldn't see his sisters. He turned around and he couldn't see his brothers. Fluffy was alone. Fluffy was lost.

Oh, how Fluffy cried! The storm didn't last very long, but when it was over he couldn't see his family anywhere. It was a rather big pond and all of the banks looked the same, so he didn't know which way his home might be.

Fluffy felt terrible. He was hungry and cold, and there was no one to feed him or get him warm. He was lonely, and there was no one to play with. He missed his family; he needed his family. He started to wish that he had minded his mother better and been nicer to his sisters. He started looking everywhere to see if he could see anyone he knew or anything he could remember.

Finally he saw an old ring-neck duck swimming by the shore. Fluffy didn't know him, but he had a kind face, so Fluffy swam over to him. "Can you help me? I'm lost," said Fluffy. The wise old duck squinted his eyes at him. "What's your name?" he asked. "Fluffy," said Fluffy. "Fluffy who?" said the wise old duck. "Ummm" (for just a minute Fluffy forgot his family name—then he remembered and he was so proud and so glad)—"it's Fluffy Honker," he said. "Oh," said the wise old duck, "are you the lucky boy with the beautiful mother and strong father?" "Yes," said Fluffy—he was excited now. "Are you the lucky lad with the six brothers and sisters?" "Yes, I am, sir," said Fluffy.

The wise old duck knew exactly where Fluffy lived, and he took him right home. Mr. and Mrs. Honker were very happy to see their lost baby. They put their wings around him and said over and over, "Thank goodness." Fluffy's brothers and sisters stood all around him and said, "Peep, peep, peep," in a very excited way.

It's very good to have a family!

V. Reading List

Aliki. *This Is My Family.* New York: Holt, Rinehart & Winston, 1963.

Bickerstaff, George. *My Special Family.* Salt Lake City: Bookcraft, 1977.

Brown, M.B. *First Night Away from Home.* New York: Franklin Watts, 1960.

Gezi, K. *Beebi, the Little Blue Bell.* Chicago: Child's World, 1976.

Hallinan, P.K. *We're Very Good Friends, My Brother and I.* Chicago: Children's Press, 1976.

Koinaiko, J., and Rosenthal, K. *Your Family Tree.* New York: Parents Magazine Press, 1963.

Miles, B. *A House for Everyone.* New York: Alfred A. Knopf, 1958.

Moncure, J. *A New Boy in Kindergarten.* Chicago: Child's World, 1977.

——————. *What Does a Koala Bear Need?* Chicago: Children's Press, 1976.

Schlein, M. *The Way Mothers Are.* Chicago: Albert Whitman & Co., 1963.

Swetnam, E. *The Day You Were Born.* Racine, Wisc.: Western Publishing Co., 1971.

Vasiliu, M. *Do You Remember?* New York: The John Day Co., 1966.

Zolotow, C. *Over and Over.* New York: Harper & Brothers, 1957.

——————. *The Sky Was Blue.* New York: Harper & Row Publishers, 1963.

——————. *Sleepy Book.* New York: Lothrop, Lee & Shepard, 1958.

VI. Postscript

A. A mother volunteered to come to a Joy School class with her baby. She talked about how much she loved the baby, and showed the children how she bathed, dressed, and fed him. Then each child had a turn to sit in the rocker and hold the baby for a moment.

When Benjamin, age three, went home, he said to his mother, "You really wanted me, didn't you? I was so cute when I was a baby and you loved me so much. Thanks for rocking me and changing my diaper."

B. Each class at the Joy School is identified by a color name: the red class, the blue class, and so on. The children develop pride in their class and feel the security of belonging to a group of their peers. Johanna joined the orange class in the middle of the year, and on her first day, Tyler took it upon himself to show her around and introduce her to the other children. He was heard to say, "You'll like the orange class. They're the 'specialist' kids in the Joy School."

Teaching the Joy of Individual Confidence and Uniqueness
12

☐ *"Ye have . . . lost the confidence of your children, because of your bad examples before them."* (*Jacob 2:35.*)

"Study [your children's] dispositions and their temperaments, and deal with them accordingly." (Discourses of Brigham Young, *p. 207.*)

No two flowers are alike, and no two children alike, yet every flower and every child is equally beautiful.

I. Examples and Description

A. *Adult:* I had a favorite professor in graduate school, a man whose every move transmitted a certain "I'm okay, you're okay" type of joy to all who were around him. He had remarkable patience. When a student could not seem to grasp a point, he would not chide or criticize; instead he would compliment the student on some other point where he was strong. He supervised a research report I did, and I came to know him well. He had some strange quirks (typical, I guess, of an absent-minded professor), such as wearing two pairs of glasses at once and occasionally walking into class in midsummer with a pair of winter galoshes on his feet. He was a small man with a bad leg that had always precluded athletics. He couldn't sing or speak well. In fact, he seemed to have few particular abilities, yet he always seemed totally self-confident—not cocky or over-bearing, just quietly of the belief that he could discuss anything, do anything. I guess he was a celebrity of sorts, because he was often in the company of other celebrities, from the governor of the State to the star right fielder of the Boston Red Sox. There was a joy in his confidence, a vigor, a lust for life. I'll never forget the day in class when he said that *fear* was the antonym of *confidence,* and *joy* was the synonym.

I did well in his class, in part because I found him so interesting, and by the end of the year I knew him well enough that we had lunch together once in a while. I asked the source of his confidence. To my surprise, he answered rather quickly, as though he had thought it through many times, almost rehearsed it. He said there were two elements, the first of which was his faith. He said he liked the word *faith* better than *confidence,* because faith implied the inputs of a higher power. He expressed to me, with no hesitation or inhibition, his belief in a higher power to whom he could pray and who he felt would guide and nudge and help him through life.

"What is the second thing?" I asked. "Well," he said, "I'm a little like the great craftsman who made the finest violins in the world. Stradivari used to say, 'The Lord can't make a Stradivarius without Antonio Stradivari.' I have certain gifts, and I think I have discovered what most of them are. I am very, very good at conceptualizing and analyzing 'production-line bottlenecks.' I am very, very good at understanding what motivates people. I am sufficiently confident in two or three basic areas that I feel equal to anyone. I am as far superior to my friend Carl in these things as he is to me at baseball. Thus, we respect each other; we see each other as totally different equals."

I've thought a great deal about what he said. His joy was confidence. His confidence was a combination of faith and self-discovered gifts. I realized that everyone can have both, that no one is precluded from faith, and no one is without particular, unique gifts.

B. *Child:* Children can feel the joy of confidence and individual uniqueness. This fact is often illustrated by children themselves at our experimental Joy School. Early in our first year, when we were dealing with the physical joys, I had an experience that taught me something about the joy of individual confidence. A group of children were dancing, and the teacher was showing them how to skip. I was sitting at the side, observing. There were about ten children, four of whom just could not grasp the technique or coordination of skipping. It intrigued me that three of the four looked dejected, embarrassed, and upset because they couldn't do it. Each of the three, in his own way, stopped trying: one cried, one walked out, and one started acting silly and boisterous to distract attention from his failure. The fourth little boy showed absolutely no embarrassment or concern or self-consciousness for not being able to skip. He kept watching, kept trying, kept failing, kept watching, kept trying. When the exercise was over, I asked him some questions:

"Do you like to skip?"

"Yes, but I can't do it very good."

"Well, did you wish they'd stop skipping and do something you were better at?"

"No, because I want to learn how."

"Do you feel bad because you can't skip?"

"No."

"Why not?"

"Because I'm better at other things."

"Like what?"

"Mommy says I'm good at painting pictures."

"I see."

"And I'm 'specially good at keeping my baby brother happy."

"I see, Jimmy. Thanks for answering my questions."

"That's all right. Don't worry, someday I'm going to be good at skipping too."

An amazing interchange for a four-year-old. But the principle behind it is not particularly amazing—it's quite natural. A person who is secure in the knowledge that he is good at certain things can much more easily accept the things he is not good at.

II. Methods

A. *Obvious, open, unconditional love.* A child who feels an inalterable parental love has a built-in foundation for confidence. He knows that no failure, no mistake, will rob him of that love and family acceptance. Tell him of your consistent love. Always separate your anger or disappointment or criticism of the thing he has done from your unchanging love for him.

B. *Know each child well as an individual.* You can't help a child build confidence around his inherent gifts and talents unless you come to know what those gifts and talents are. Two ways to learn: (1) in private chats with the child, time spent together watching and appreciating; and (2) in organized time, spent as husband and wife, discussing each child, sharing perceptions, taking notes, discovering together more about the personality and individual character of each child. In our family, we call this kind of discussion a "five-facet review." It consists of simply getting together as husband and wife (perhaps while going out to dinner) and discussing each child individually, one at a time. We ask ourselves, How is he doing physically? How is he doing mentally? How is he doing emotionally? Then we proceed through each facet for each child, asking ourselves if he is experiencing each of the fifteen joys in this book. It is remarkable how much parents can learn from each other's observations.

C. *Genuinely respect each child and his own gifts.* Our children are really our brothers and sisters—as old as we, coeternal with us, quite possibly more advanced in an eternal perspective than we are. With this thought in mind, sometimes it becomes a bit easier to (1) show an added measure of faith in them after any kind of failure; (2) discuss our own failures with them and tell them what we learned from each; (3) praise their accomplishments lavishly and honestly, particularly accomplishments in areas where we perceive special aptitude; and (4) never criticize or tear the children down personally. We should criticize instead the bad things they have done, making sure they still know our total love for them. Never criticize in public—"praise in public, correct in private."

D. *Independence, self-reliance, responsibility at an early age.* Confidence and its joy tie directly into being able to do useful things. Each child should have a job in the family, for the family—particularly daily or weekly jobs—for which he is praised and made to feel very able and very important, very much a key part of the family.

Another way to build responsibility is to let children make their own decisions whenever possible—what to wear, what to do on Saturday morning—and then to praise their judgment.

*E. *Teaching and establishing the fact that everyone is different.*

The Rock Game: Blindfold the children and give them each a rock. (Use widely different sizes and shapes.) Have them feel the rocks very carefully, getting to know what their particular rocks are like. Then put the rocks in the center of the circle and take the blindfolds off. Let each child find his own rock. Teach the children that everything God has made is unique: no two rocks are the same, no two flowers, no two leaves. All people are different too. Some are good at one thing, some at another, but Heavenly Father loves us all the same, regardless of what we are good at.

F. *Help children to see what their own unique gifts are—and that these gifts are as good as anyone else's.*

*1. The "One Thing I Like About You" game: Sit five or six children in a circle, with one in the middle. Let each child say something he likes about the one in the middle, such as "One thing I like about Tommy is that he can tie his own shoes."

*2. Individual profile charts: Trace a profile from each child's shadow on a poster. Then, under each profile, write in the eye color, hair color, sex, age, position in the family, and what the child is good at. Put the posters up on the wall and let each child take pride in his uniqueness.

*G. *Make a book about the child.* Help each child to make a book about himself. You might use wallpaper samples for decorative covers. Suggested title: *All About Me* or *I Am Special.* Suggested pages:

1. Child's name, decorated with sparkles and colors.
2. Profile or picture of child.
3. Family information, such as number of brothers and sisters and child's position in family.

4. Personal information—age, birthdate, height, weight, eye color, hair color, best friend, favorite food, favorite color.

5. "Who loves me" list, with the last entry reading, "I love me too."

6. A handprint (made with fingerpaint or ink).

7. A footprint.

8. A painting by the child.

9. "Favorite things" pictures (food, toys, activities) cut from magazines and pasted in.

10. A list of things the child is good at.

*H. *Pin a badge on the child* that says "I am John and I'm special."

I. *Help each child to be secure in his own uniqueness.*

*1. Multiple answer games: Who are you? (The children respond with their self-perceptions—an artist, a tricycle rider, a dancer, a skipper.) Who loves you? (Teacher, parents, grandparents, brothers and sisters, the milkman.) The process builds a long list of reassurance and confidence.

*2. The "which is better" game: Ask children which is better: blue eyes or brown, to be an artist or a baseball player, and so on. The answer is always, "They're both just as good."

J. *An exclusive club for each child.* "Nothing makes a child feel more special than to share something with a parent that none of the other children (or the other parent) are included in. We have four such clubs in our family; each has only two members—Daddy and one child. Saren and Daddy's club is "The Literary Discussion Club." (They discuss books in a very grown-up way.) Shawni and Daddy's is "The Brown Eyes Club." (They are the only ones in the family who have brown eyes. Their club has a secret handshake and password.) Josh and Daddy's is "The Train, Boat, Airplane, Race Car, Go-cart Club." (The name is self-explanatory.) Saydi and Daddy's is "The Smile Club." (Saydi was only two when this club started, and smiling was what she did best.) There is a feeling of specialness, of uniqueness, of exclusivity, that makes children more aware of their individual worth.

K. *Special nicknames for each child.* A similar feeling of specialness comes with an affectionate nickname, especially when it is used exclusively by one parent. To Daddy, Saren is "Princess," Shawni is "Pixie," Josh is "Herkimer," Saydi is "Sugar Plum," Jonah is "Boomer Bumpkin," and Talmadge is "Mudgie." Each perhaps feels a little more special because of it.

L. *Mommy and Daddy dates.* Set aside a special time each week when there is a one-to-one relationship between mother or father (or both) and one child. These occasions may sometimes take planning, and other times they may consist simply of maximizing the moment.

M. *"Empty Books."* A dear friend mentioned at the time our first two children were still tiny that she got a great deal of satisfaction from buying an "empty book" (well-bound with empty pages) for each child when he was a baby and recording special events and character changes in the child's life as he grew. The ultimate plan was to present it to him on his wedding day.

We have followed her example and have found many benefits that we hadn't planned. The children know we are keeping the books and they feel a great sense of uniqueness and pride in knowing that even though, for the most part, the contents are secret until their wedding day, they themselves are individuals in their parents' eyes. They see us writing about those special events and are secretly thrilled that we take time for just *them.* Also, in reading back over events from these first few years, we realize how easily we forget those momentous moments (birth, toddler's mischief, starting school) in a child's life unless they are recorded. They'll make great "vicarious journals" and will be lots of fun for our children's children to read some day. Reading back through them is also, for us, a good chance to evaluate and analyze the progress and needs of each child.

N. *A little, private "chest" for each child.* Give each child a wooden box with some kind of lock. Let it be his very own place to keep little special private things, from ribbons to marbles, from jewelry pins to keys to wind the toy train. Then, as parents, respect the privacy of each child's chest. In our family, we made the treasure chests together from plywood in our "workshop." Each child painted his own.

III. Family Focal Point: Family Experts Board

Each child has unique gifts. The challenge is one of identifying them and reinforcing them. A useful tool is a "family experts board." Rule off a large mounted sheet into sixteen four-inch squares. Within each square put a picture of a family member doing something he is good at. This started in our family one family home evening night when we decided to talk about the things in which each child excelled. At first the answers were not obvious or readily apparent to us, and we realized that we didn't know our children as well as we should.

A child's age doesn't matter. We made our first family experts board when Saydi was only six months old, but she was listed as the family expert in several important categories: "noticing," "waving bye-bye," "making loud noises." As the children grew older, the board began to change; the real gifts, those things that can breed the joy of individual uniqueness and confidence, began to emerge and surface on the board. Saren, at age five, had on her list "creative dance," "playing the violin," and "being friendly to strangers." Shawni, at age four, had "singing right on tune," "sharing," "skipping," and "counting and doing sums."

Children can draw in the board's squares illustrations of each area of expertise, such as a girl playing the piano or a boy running. As parents and children focus regularly on the gifts that should be listed on the chart, they begin to identify and reinforce those qualities that give their children the lifetime gift of joy.

IV. Story: "The Ping Pong Ball and the Christmas Tree Bulb"

Once upon a'time, at Christmastime, there were two friends. One was a Ping-Pong ball and the other was a Christmas tree bulb. Late each night, after the people in the house went to bed, the ball and the bulb used to talk. (They could talk to each other easily because the Christmas tree was right beside the Ping-Pong table.) Even though they were friends, they were jealous of each other. The Ping-Pong ball would say to the Christmas tree bulb: "Bulb, you are so lucky. You just hang there all day and people look at you and say how pretty you are. I spend the whole day getting hit with a paddle." The bulb would say, "You're the one who's lucky. All day you get to play with the children; they hold you and pat you and have fun with you. I just hang, hang, hang. No one ever touches me or plays with me."

On Christmas Eve, when Santa came, he had one of his magic elves with him. The elf heard what the ball and the bulb were saying. He said to them, "Would you like to change places?" They both said yes, and with one wave of his hand, the elf turned the ball into a bulb and the bulb into a ball. Just before the elf went up the chimney with Santa he said, "The only way you can change back into what you were is to get very, very wet."

At first the bulb was happy being a ball. The children picked him up and played with him—but he got dizzy from flying through the air, and soon he missed his tree branch. He wanted to be back there doing what he was supposed to do: hanging nice and still, and looking pretty.

The ball was happy for a few minutes being a bulb. He enjoyed being shiny and bright. After a while, though, he got bored. His neck hurt from hanging on the tree, and he missed the children and the paddles. He realized that he was meant to be a Ping-Pong ball; he was good at that and not good at being a bulb. Both of them were sad. They wanted to be themselves again. Soon they were both wishing that someone would throw water on them so they could change back. They got more and more sad. Finally they got so sad that they started to cry. Their tears got them wet, and suddenly they changed back into themselves.

V. Reading List

Behrens, June. *Who Am I?* Chicago: Children's Press, 1968.

Berger, T. *I Have Feelings.* New York: Human Science Press, 1971.

Charlip, R. *Hooray for Me.* New York: Parents Magazine Press, 1975.

Freeman, D. *Dandelion.* New York: Viking Press, 1964.

Friskey, M. *Rackety, That Very Special Rabbit.* Chicago: Children's Press, 1976.

Hallinan, P. K. *I'm Glad to Be Me.* Chicago: Children's Press, 1977.

Hoff, S. *Ida the Bareback Rider.* New York: G. P. Putnam's Sons, 1972.

Johnston, M. *Sing Me a Song.* Chicago: Child's World, 1977.

Kent, J. *Just Only John.* New York: Parents Magazine Press, 1968.

Larris, A. *People Are Like Lollipops.* New York: Holiday House, 1971.

Moncure, J. *Try on a Shoe.* Chicago: Child's World, 1976.

Slobodkin, L. *Millions and Millions and Millions.* New York: Vanguard Press, 1955.

Seuss, Dr. "The Sneetches" from *The Sneetches and Other Stories.* New York: Random House, 1961.

Wulf, K. *I'm Glad I'm Little.* Chicago: Child's World, 1977.

VI. Postscript

A. Saren, four and a half, and Shawni, three, were drawing on the blackboard. Saren had drawn quite a detailed picture of a little girl, including eyebrows and eyelashes, dress, shoes, and ribbon in hair. Shawni had drawn a simple face with arms and legs coming out of the sides and bottom of the head. Saren viewed Shawni's picture and, confident in her own artistic ability, did not criticize it, but instead said, "Shawni, that's very good for a three-year-old, but don't you remember we have tummies?"

B. We were discussing how no two persons are exactly alike. One child, pointing to Travis and Terry, identical twins who had recently started school and who both had many behavior problems, said, "These two are." Then Danielle countered with, "No, they aren't. Travis hits when he gets mad and Terry cries."

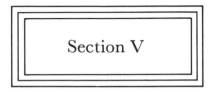

SOCIAL JOYS

"The Church is an aid to the training of children; so also is the state, but neither is supreme. . . . The home is the center of civilization, and the responsibilities of the home rest upon the parents of the home. . . . The greatest trust that can come to a man and woman is the placing in their keeping the life of a little child." (David O. McKay, Stepping Stones, *p. 301.*)

"Every home has both body and spirit. You may have a beautiful house with all the decorations that modern art can give or wealth bestow. You may have all the outward forms that will please the eye and yet not have a home. It may be a hovel, a log hut, a tent, a wickiup, if you have the right spirit within, the true love of Christ, and love for one another . . . you have the true life of the home." (David O. McKay, Stepping Stones, *p. 288.*)

Preserving the Joy of Realness, Honesty, and Candor

13

□ *"What did you promise your little girl if she would do so and so? Did you promise her a present for well doing? 'Yes.' Have you recollected it? 'No, it has gone from my mind,' says the mother. If she does ill have you promised her a chastisement? 'Yes,' Did you keep your word? You have not, and the child forms the conclusion in its own mind that the mother tells that which is not true—she says she will do this or that, and she does not do it."* (Discourses of Brigham Young, *p. 210.*)

I. Examples and Description

A. *Child:* Children are born with the gift of realness, congruence, honesty, candor. At first, they know nothing else. People have to learn to be false, to cover up feelings, to lie. Josh just turned three and hasn't learned to do any of them yet. Last time I tried to give him a bath, the big new shampoo bottle was empty. "Did you dump it out, Josh?" His brow furrowed as he anticipated the worst, but a lie never occurred to him. "Yes, Dad." We have a family law against "dumping" and Josh knows the law, so he needed a little punishment. But I praised him so much for telling the truth that it outbalanced the punishment.

As Josh splashed in the bath, my mind went back to another time when the shampoo was dumped, when Saren was five and Shawni four. "Did you do it, Saren?" Her look showed that she was about to say, "No, Shawni did." Then a change came to her eye. "Daddy, sometimes it's hard to tell the truth, isn't it." I felt inner rejoicing. She had consciously chosen truth over a lie.

Josh pulled me back to the present. "Daddy, dry me off!" As I dried Josh, I had candor and honesty on my mind and happened to hear Saren, now six, in whom we had tried so hard to preserve that quality. She was in her bedroom with a new friend from school. They were discussing dolls.

Saren: "This doll has a problem. Her skirt has lost its elastic so it slips right off."

Friend: "Let's tie a string around it."

(Silence for several minutes)

Saren: "It scares me when Miss Christie calls on me to read in school. Does it scare you?"

Friend: "A little."

Saren: "I'm getting over it, though."

Friend: "The more you do it, the easier it is."

Saren: "I guess so. There, we got the skirt almost ready."

(Pause)

Friend: "Saren, do you like me?"

Saren: "Of course, silly, I like everything about you."

Friend: "Everything?"

Saren: "Except I didn't like it when you played with Patty at recess—but Mommy says I was just jealous."

Friend: "What's jealous?"

Saren: "Not wanting someone to have more fun than you."

Friend: "I like you too, Saren."

To be honest, to be open, to talk freely about the real feelings—what a joy!

What a need there is to reinforce children in their natural honesty, to get across to the clean slate of their minds the fact that it is just as all right to be sad or mad as to be glad, that what really counts is being real.

Congruence, in a psychological sense, is a matching up of how you really feel, how you think you feel, and how you say you feel. Straightforward honesty and candor, added to congruence, can free and lift the mind into the clear realm, void of "games" and "fronts" and "stiff upper lips." Grown-ups, too, can find this congruence.

B. *Adult:* I watched a local political race with more than usual interest one year because my friend John was a surprise candidate. John was a surprise because he seemed so unpolitical. He was the most honest and candid man I knew, and my first thought was, "He's too honest to make the promises that win elections."

I was right about John, but wrong about the result. John was brutally honest, and he enjoyed people's surprised reaction to his unbending truthfulness. He disagreed with many of the people he was supposed to agree with. He said no to people who weren't used to hearing the word. He said "I don't know" when he didn't know.

A week before the election, John was calm and seemingly unaffected, unlike the many on-edge politicians I had known. "Don't you care if you win?" I asked him. "Maybe not," he said, "at least not in the way you mean. I've been straight on every point. If I win, the real me wins. If I lose, I'm still the real me. I'd rather be the real loser than the unreal winner." John won. I was happily surprised.

There is power in utter candor, and joy in simply saying what you really think, in being right with self and with others and with God. The freedom of a clear conscience is endless.

II. Methods

A. *Example.* Be as real and congruent as your children are. Sharing your example (or following theirs) is the strongest possible reinforcement. Verbalize your real feelings, fears, and insecurities as well as your joys and loves. Show control, but show honesty! Tell them how you feel— "I'm upset about what happened this afternoon, so I got more angry with you than I should have." Never let them hear you lie about anything to anyone.

Forsake the false parental notions of not arguing when they're there, and not punishing when you are angry or upset. Certainly there is a need for control, but be genuine. It's all right to show some honest indignation, and it's all right for children to see a parental disagreement as long as (1) the light of love shines through, (2) it's not about them (the children), and (3) you make up afterwards—and they *see* that you do.

B. *Reinforcement and praise.* Since children start with realness, congruence, and honesty, recognition and reinforcement become the two great keys. Whatever they get attention for, they'll probably do again; whatever they get praise for, they'll very likely do again; whatever they get joy and praise out of, they'll almost certainly do again. Encourage them to always tell how they feel—to tell not only you but also other family members, school teachers, friends, or even Primary teachers.

Psychiatrists tell us that it's usually as hard to get a person to know *how* he really feels as it is to help him know *why* he feels that way. The reason it is so hard to know how we feel is that we stop so early in life telling anyone, even ourselves, how we really feel. We need to recognize emotions, accept them, and, if possible, enjoy them.

C. *Show acceptability of letting our feelings show.*

*1. Show pictures from magazines of children and grown-ups crying. Ask: "What made them cry?" "Is it okay?" Respond: "Sure! Crying helps to get the sad and the mad out. Just be careful not to cry without a reason."

2. Have an acceptable way for a child to show and vent his anger—a big punching bag or pillow or inflatable figure.

3. Ask often, "How did that make you feel?" Then really listen!

Oh, how children teach us! Just now, as I write, five-year-old Saren has a question. I give her a too-quick, ask-it-later answer. She says, "Dad, when you say that, it makes me feel like you don't care about me . . . you only care about your book." I put down the book, praise her, answer her.

4. Point out mistakes others make in *not* telling what bothers them (in stories or real life or television shows). Show how it would have been better if they had told.

5. Have a pact and a family tradition to always tell the truth. Make the reward for honesty psychologically outweigh the punishment for the admitted wrong.

*6. Pantomime certain emotions, such as sadness, anger, and happiness.

III. Family Focal Point: Happys and Sads

Bedtime is a good time for a little honest, important dialogue between parent and child. Years ago we started a tradition of asking each child as he was tucked in, "What was your 'happy' and your 'sad' today?" Children like to think back through the day, to recognize and talk about emotions. "My happy was when my friend came over to play," or "when I got two desserts," or "when I jumped in the leaf pile," or "when Daddy came home." "My sad was when Lisa wouldn't play with me at school," or "when I couldn't hop very good in hopscotch," or "when I cut my finger," or "I didn't have any sads today."

The answers open up quick, golden chances to talk about real feelings. "How did it feel to play with Susan?" "Why do you suppose Lisa wouldn't play? Did something sad happen to her?" "Did you feel that someone else was better at hopscotch than you?" "What can you do better than they?"

IV. Story: "Isabel's Little Lie"

One day Isabel told a little lie. She wasn't supposed to feed her dinner to her dog, Barker, but she did, and when her mother came in and saw her plate all clean, Isabel said that she had eaten it all. (That was a little lie, wasn't it?) The dinner was chicken, and Barker got a little bone in his throat and pretty soon he started to cough and snort and act very uncomfortable.

"Do you know what's wrong with Barker?" asked Mother. "No," said Isabel. (That was another lie, wasn't it? But Isabel *had* to do it so her mother wouldn't know she told the first lie.) Mother looked in Barker's mouth but couldn't see anything. "Did Barker eat something, Isabel?" "I don't know, Mommy." (That was another lie, wasn't it? But she didn't want her mother to know about the first two lies.)

Barker got worse, and Mother took him to the dog hospital. Isabel went too. "What happened to the dog?" asked the doctor. "We don't know," said Isabel. (That was another lie, wasn't it? But if Isabel had told, then Mother and the dog doctor would know she had lied before.) The dog doctor said, "If it's just a bone, we could get it out with an instrument, but it might be glass, so we may have to operate."

Isabel decided it was time to tell the truth. She said, "It's a bone, and I *did* know Barker ate it, and I *didn't* eat all my dinner, and I *did* give it to Barker, and I won't tell lies any more, because if you tell one you might have to tell more and more." Isabel started to cry, but her mother loved her, and she decided she really would tell the truth from then on.

V. Reading List

Behrens, J. *How I Feel.* Chicago: Children's Press, 1973.

Berger, T. *I Have Feelings.* New York: Human Sciences Press, 1971.

Brown, M. *First Night Away from Home.* New York: Funk & Wagnalls, 1960.

Erickson, P. *Stand Tall.* Salt Lake City: Hawkes Publishing Co., 1978.

Helena, A. *The Lie.* Chicago: Children's Press, 1977.

How Do You Feel. Chicago: Child's World, 1973.

Keates, E. *Peter's Chair.* New York: Harper & Row Publishers, 1967.

Riley, S. *What Does It Mean? Afraid.* Chicago: Child's World, 1978.

_____. *What Does It Mean? Angry.* Chicago: Child's World, 1978.

Sendak, M. *Where the Wild Things Are.* New York: Harper & Row Publishers, 1963.

Thompson, V. *Sad Day, Glad Day.* New York: Scholastic Book Services, 1962.

Whitney, A. M. *Just Awful.* Massachusetts: Addison, Wesley Publishing Co., 1971.

Zolotow, C. *If It Weren't for You.* New York: Harper & Row Publishers, 1966.

_____. *The Night When Mother Went Away.* New York: Lothrop, Lee & Shepard, 1958.

VI. Postscript

A. Aaron is four. His grandmother, who sometimes picks him up from Joy School, told this experience: She had been tending Aaron and his brother and sisters. She was tired and got upset with the children for something they had done. She yelled at them crossly. When things calmed down, Aaron came to her and said, "Grandma, you were really angry, weren't you? And yelling at us helped you get the mad out. But I know you still love us even when you yell." Later that evening, when his little sister got angry and hit him, Aaron explained to her, "Melissa, it's all right to hit things, but not people. Here, you can hit this pillow."

B. Sammy, age three, fell in the play yard and scraped his elbow. He began to cry loudly, and other children gathered around to see what was the matter. Jodi, four, put her arm around him and, quoting from a song they had learned in school, announced to the other children as well as to Sammy, "It's all right to cry. Crying gets the sad out of you."

Teaching the Joy of Communication and Relationships 14

☐ *"In my experience I have learned that the greatest difficulty that exists in the little bickerings and strifes of man with man, woman with woman, children with children, parents with children, brothers with sisters, and sisters with brothers, arises from the want of rightly understanding each other."* (Discourses of Brigham Young, *p. 203.*)

I. Examples and Description

A. *Adult:* I once knew a middle-aged man, an accountant, who had a ledger-book-sized Christmas card list. In his thick book all the pages were filled; there were hundreds and hundreds of names. "Business contacts?" I asked. He glanced over, paused for a moment as though considering whether he should tell me something pretty important, then said, "No, they're relationships." He anticipated my next question and went on in his accounting terminology: "Every relationship you form, no matter how small, if it is genuine, can be an asset of eternal duration. No other entry can cancel it out. Some of us spend all our time on temporary assets: money, positions, achievements. We ought to spend more on the eternal assets like relationships. Whenever I earn one, I make an entry on my Christmas card list."

I watched the accountant closer from then on, and found that he practiced what he preached. When he met someone—on a plane, in his business, at a PTA meeting—his attitude seemed to be: "What can I learn from you? What is interesting and unique about you?" For him, life was a fascinating kaleidoscope of relationships, of endless people, each endlessly interesting and each offering more potential inner joy than a new car or a new position.

B. *Child:* For little children, particularly those with strong self-images, genuine relationships are easy. Friends came by the other night, a business acquaintance and his wife. The four of us sat in the parlor, playing self-conscious "I" games: "How can *I* impress them?" "What can we talk

about that *I* know a lot about?" "How can *I* seem sophisticated and 'with it'?"

Meanwhile, their five-year-old daughter went upstairs
to play with our daughter of the same age. Their discussion
(I caught part of it when I went up to get some papers) was
more mature than ours because it was real, honest, open,
and without ulterior motives. "Janet, you should bring
your pajamas next time you come. No one uses the bottom
bunk bed, so we could sleep in the same room." "Will your
mommy care if I do?" "No, she likes your mommy."
"Good, because I like you." When it was time to go, they
came downstairs holding hands, smiling, friends, as if
they'd known each other for years.

II. *Methods*

A. *General*

1. Develop a tradition of listening. Really listen—use
psychologist Karl Rogers's technique of not directing the
conversation, but just acknowledging what children say
and agreeing, letting them go on. Help children glimpse
the joy of seeing the other person's point of view.

2. Have a sense of humor. Show how "crisis plus time
usually equals humor." Laugh at your own mistakes, and
laugh with children at every opportunity.

3. Always encourage children to hug and make up
after a disagreement.

4. Show romantic love between parents: holding
hands, kissing as you leave, opening the car door, sitting
close together on car seat, avoiding harsh words, emphasiz-
ing loving words.

5. Teach and explain the Golden Rule.

6. Role reversal: let the children play parents and you
play child, so they see and appreciate your problems.

B. *Communicate*

1. Speak candidly, graphically, logically to children.

2. Help children write letters—you write what they
express. Praise them for saying and phrasing things well.

3. Give lavish praise whenever they explain or say anything particularly well.

4. At dinner, encourage a child to talk about something that he knows a lot about—perhaps something he has just learned and is proud to know.

5. Talk on the phone with children whenever possible.

6. Encourage children to take advantage of any speaking opportunities that are available to them in church or school. Help them really communicate to an audience.

7. Try to avoid communicating *for* children—and don't give them a cue every time they are supposed to speak. Don't say, "Say thank you," or "What do you say, dear?"

*8. Discuss the fact that people are the only ones who can communicate with words—they don't have to fight like animals. Say "Let's talk about it," whenever a conflict comes up.

C. *Relationships*

1. Make their first relationship with you a truly beautiful one.

*2. Talk out disagreements. Sit them down face to face to work out problems or disagreements they have with each other.

3. Be an example. Show that relationships should be more important than achievements by always taking time for a relationship (even when in the middle of an achievement).

4. Don't always step in on children's relationships or try to steer them too much—let them work things out. (My children were having a terrific fight in the back seat of our station wagon once when I had laryngitis. I found that they worked it out better on their own than they would have with my direction.)

*5. Role-play relationship problems and let the children give ways to solve particular difficulties. Role-play how and what to do if you want a toy someone else has, or if you hurt someone, or if you both want to be the mommy when you play house, or if someone calls you a naughty name. Have children act out a situation that ended in unhappiness and show how it could have been handled better and ended happily.

6. Encourage children to have their own special friends over to play. (Sometimes this requires having other children play elsewhere for a while so that one child feels he has control of the situation.)

7. Do something special for your children to stress the importance of your friendship with them. Take them for a drive, or bring them a surprise.

8. Strive to develop the family as a social unit. Encourage children to think of family members as their best friends. At first they may have to be told, as the following conversation illustrates:

Mother: "Josh, who's your best friend?"

Josh: "Christopher."

Mother: "But who is the friend you play with *most* of the time and the one who makes you laugh when she plays peek-a-boo?"

Josh: "Oh, Saydi."

Mother: "That's right."

9. Help children to identify and understand the feelings of others: "Why do you suppose she seems so unfriendly today? Maybe she doesn't feel well. Maybe someone was unfriendly to her."

*10. Make a little booklet of "kind words" with a child. Let him paste in the words:

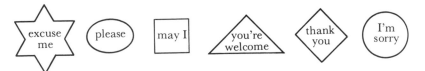

*11. Play the game "Which is the best way?" in which children act out a good and bad way of deciding who should have the first turn, getting the dishes done after Sunday dinner, getting ready for school in the morning, or deciding which television show to watch.

III. Family Focal Point: "Guess Who's Coming to Dinner"

When Saren was four, she went through a short but painful phase of "I don't have any friends." She seemed shy in nursery school, not her normal, initiative-taking self. Then one day she asked if she could invite a friend over for dinner. Of course we ,were glad—a "breakthrough" perhaps? It was more than that. Something about having a friend in her home, to see her house and family, seemed to wipe the shyness right away.

Ever since then, we have had one special supper each week when one family member, on a rotating basis, parents included, has a friend over for the evening meal. It shows children how important relationships are, and it exposes them to strangers, to interesting people, some of whom are very different from them. It puts the premium where it should be: on the joy of communication and relationships.

IV. Story—"Herman Finds a Friend"

Herman was a baby bird. He had a mother who brought him worms to eat in their small nest in the big sycamore tree. He had learned to fly. He had pretty blue feathers. Nest, mother, worms, blue feathers, air to fly in— he had everything to make him happy, right?

Then why was Herman sad?

He didn't even know why, but he was.

Then one day another bird's nest was built on the next highest limb of the tree. A new bird family, the Robin Redbreasts, moved in. They had a boy bird just Herman's age named Reginald. Herman and Reginald flew together, played together, explored together. Herman wasn't unhappy anymore.

What made the difference?

V. Reading List

Ets, M. H. *Talking Without Words.* New York: The Viking Press, 1968.

Guilfoile, E. *Nobody Listens to Andrew*. Chicago: Follett Publishing Co., 1957.

Hallinan, P. K. *That's What a Friend Is*. Chicago: Children's Press, 1977.

Hook, F. *My Book of Friends*. Cincinnati: Standard Publishing Co., 1968.

Penn, R. B. *Mommies Are for Loving*. New York: G. P. Putnam's Sons, 1962.

Riley, S. *What Does It Mean? Sorry*. Chicago: Children's Press, 1978.

Udry, J. M. *Let's Be Enemies*. New York: Harper & Brothers, 1961.

_____. *Next Door to Laura Linda*. Chicago: Albert Whitman & Co., 1965.

Zolotow, C. *Big Sister and Little Sister*. New York: Harper & Row Publishers, 1966.

_____. *Do You Know What I'll Do?* New York: Harper & Row Publishers, 1958.

_____. *My Friend John*. New York: Harper & Row Publishers, 1968.

_____. *The Quarreling Book*. New York: Harper & Row Publishers, 1963.

VI. *Postscript*

A. Meredith, Michael, and Kevin were in the playroom putting on dress-up clothes. Michael and Kevin both wanted the same jacket and tie. They were hitting and pulling as each declared in a loud voice, "I'm the daddy." Then Meredith spoke up. "Let's talk about it," she said as she took another jacket from the hook. In a minute they had it all worked out and everyone was happy. Kevin would be the daddy and Michael would be the uncle. Meredith, the mediator, was only four years old.

B. One day Mac, five, accidentally knocked down the house that Andrew, four, had built with the large blocks.

Andrew: "Hey, watch out!"

Mac: "I'm sorry. I'll help you build it again."

Andrew (with a smile): "You're forgiven."

Teaching
the Joy
of Sharing
and
Service

15

□ *"Ye will teach them [children] to love one another, and to serve one another."* (*Mosiah 4:15.*)

I. Examples and Description

A. *Adult:* I have a friend who taught me a lesson about joy. He is a public person: that is, the public knows him. (I would guess that 50 percent of all persons in the western world recognize his name, 95 percent of those interested in sports.) One conversation we had drifted to pleasure. What did we do with our spare time? What did we do with those rare moments—rarer for him than for me—that we really had to ourselves? (Keep in mind, he could do anything, go anywhere, have anything that money could buy.) He said, "When I have a moment for myself, I try to use it to find some way to help someone. That's where I find real happiness. It's so much more fun than doing something for yourself."

I'd heard that you can judge a man by what he does with his spare time. I used that criteria and judged this man as being great; maybe more importantly, I judged him to be joyful, because the joy of giving is so great. We know that is true, or should know it, because it was taught by the greatest giver of all time, in the meridian of time. (It's interesting how, as I write, the words *give* and *great* keep knotting together.)

"He that loseth his life shall find it." The joy comes from losing one's self in helping others, from dismissing self-worries to make room for other-worries. We make our living by what we get, but we make our life by what we give. Emerson said, "See how the masses of men worry themselves into nameless graves . . . while, here and there, a great, unselfish soul forgets himself into immortality."

I was traveling on business, two full days away, meetings all day, free evenings. The first night I treated myself (hard day, I deserved it) to the finest meal at the finest restaurant. I went to bed satisfied, dulled. The next evening on my way to the same spot, I noticed a blind man sitting with his dog in front of a little shop, selling baskets he had made. I stopped, talked for an hour, bought a basket and a stool, cheered him up, listened to him, learned from him. ("I've lost one sense and gained four," he said.) I told him that I liked his company, liked him as a friend, that I'd be back. I saw tears in his blind eyes as we shook hands. I went to bed that night thrilled, tingling—and, in a small but deep sort of way, a better man.

B. *Child:* On the Christmas when Saren was four and Shawni was three, we tried something. Starting in the fall, they began to "earn" their own money by doing extra household chores. Each got a new piggy bank "for deposit only." I was amazed at the anticipation of a three-year-old and how anxious she was to "buy my own presents for people with my own 'earned money.'" That year, there were two Christmas days. One was on the twenty-third of December when we went to the variety store and the girls picked out a teacup for Grandma, measuring spoons for Mommy, and a tennis ball for three-year-old Josh (because "he can start thinking about how to hit it"). They watched the check-out clerk count their nickels and pennies. They carried their carefully concealed treasures up to their rooms and wrapped them themselves. All the while they were anticipating the joy of giving, sharing, making others happy; the feelings grew and became real from within. "Won't Grandpa be happy when he sees this?" "What will Mommy say when she opens this?"

When Christmas day came, the reactions were remarkable. The children were still grateful for their own dolls and filled stockings, but we saw real joy in the four-year-old's face when Grandma opened her cup and said, "Oh, Saren, just what I needed. I'll drink my Postum out of it every morning and think of you." There was a tear in the four-year-old's eye and a choke of real joy in her voice when Saren said, "I saved up and picked it out for you, Grandma, because I love you." Since then, we've thought back countless times: "Wasn't it fun when Josh opened his ball? Didn't that make us happy?" Children can feel the joy of sharing and service, and when they feel it, they want it again—and when they want it again, they've learned it.

We took a group of children to an old folks' home to put on a program, to pass out little gifts they had made, and to share their love. We explained, "These are old people without grandchildren to love them." I wish I had a picture of one three-year-old on an eighty-year-old's knee, arms around the neck, tears in all four eyes. And the joy of reflection afterward, as one four-year-old said to another, "We made the grandpas and grandmas happy, didn't we?" "Yes, and they made me happy." "Let's do it again."

A personal recollection (Linda's) may further illustrate the joy:

"I remember that a particularly miserable time in my life came when I was in the sixth grade. I was eleven years old, considered my leftover baby fat anything but cute, and wore salmon-colored 'cat-eye' glasses which I abhorred. I sensed that I had no style and, worst of all, thought I had no friends. I was worried about who liked me and who didn't, and each day I wondered whether or not the one marginal friend I thought I had would be nice to me.

"One Saturday afternoon while I was getting ready for a school party, I began telling my mother my feelings. I don't remember whether I just had not bothered to tell them to her before or whether she had passed them off lightly as childish whims when I had mentioned them. On this particular day, however, she took me seriously and could see that I was really concerned. As I donned my party clothes, I said, 'Mom, sometimes I feel so left out when I'm with other people. I just can't think of anything to say and yet I feel so uncomfortable if no one talks to me.'

"My mom, in her wisdom, gave me some counsel in those next few minutes that changed my life: 'Linda, whenever you are with a group of people who are socializing with one another, look around; just stand back and look around for a few minutes, and you will almost always see someone who needs you, someone who is feeling insecure and in need of a friend. You can tell by a look in the eye, a nervous mannerism, someone off by herself. Decide who needs *you* and then go to *them;* relate to them, ask questions about them, show them you care! '

"This advice was like a miracle drug for my ailing soul. I went to the party. I stood back and observed. 'There she is,' I thought as I saw Beverly, the girl with the stringy hair and the buck teeth, sweet but not too bright. Everyone knew that she lived in a strange, broken-down house outside of town with about nine brothers and sisters, equally untidy and shabby. I remember her as though it were yesterday, sitting quietly in a chair, looking at her hands, while those around her giggled and chattered and ignored her. *But what will everyone think?* I cringed in my immature mind. *If I talk to her, everyone will think I'm dumb and 'out of it' like she is.* But my conscience told me it was right, so I walked over to her. Suddenly instead of muddling in my own misery because I didn't have any friends, I became *her* friend. I started by asking questions about her family and farm, and as the party wore on, I felt her warm acceptance and saw the joy in her eyes as she understood that somebody cared about her. But even more important to me, *I* was needed. I was providing a service to someone that, in time, made me grow to appreciate her. I also noticed that no one shunned me because of my association with her.

"The experience gave me such a good feeling that I tried to pick out those who needed someone in other situations, from the schoolroom to the Sunday School class. As I began to forget myself in other people, I found that I was surrounded by a host of friends who really liked me for what I was.

"If I could instill this in our children at an even younger age, how great their rewards would be. So often we say 'Oh, they're too young to understand.' I wonder. Try teaching this principle to a four-year-old—you might be surprised."

II. Methods

A. *By example.* Oh, how children learn by what their parents do! Help an old woman with her bags. Take any opportunity to help someone while your children are with you. Build a family reputation for service and for helping. Always stop to help: people in distress, people out of gas, people looking for directions. Let your children see that helping other people is the thing to do.

Indoctrinate children with a serving orientation: "Where much is given, much *service* is expected." Teach children that the gifts and talents they have been given are there to allow them to help other people—to serve. Teach them that God gives us talents so that we might help our brothers and sisters.

B. *Help the less fortunate.*

1. Sponsor a child. The "Christian Children's Fund" and similar organizations give opportunities at a moderate cost to feel the joy of sharing with others who are in real need. Let children miss a meal once a month and send the money to a sponsored child; the organization will send pictures and letters of appreciation from the child. The joy of gratitude can intermingle here with the joy of service.

2. Help children who don't have strong families. Perhaps an orphan's home nearby allows children to go on picnics with families. Is there a neighbor child who doesn't have a happy family life? Could you include him in your family activity? Let the children feel the happiness of giving happiness.

C. *Serving each other within the family.*

1. In the Book of Mormon, King Benjamin teaches us to teach our children to serve each other. It is through service that we learn to love—isn't that why we love our children so much? Serving increases love. We have read Mosiah 2:17 to our children so many times that they call

good turns "services." ("Services" include anything from helping Josh find his socks to letting sister use the new crayons.) If we want children to love, we must teach them to serve. Older children can serve their younger brothers and sisters in countless ways.

2. Let children serve you. Make little comments like, "Oh, the paper is on the porch and I am so tired." "I can't pull these boots off." "I can't hold this leaf bag open while I dump the leaves in." "My arms are full; now how am I going to get in this door?" It's better when they volunteer to help than when you ask them directly.

D. *Doing good deeds together.*

*1. Help a needy family anonymously on Christmas. Have each child sacrifice a toy, and plan a way to get the toys under the family's tree without their knowledge.

2. Do "secret good turns." Watch for people in need, and plan for ways to make them happier. Have discussions with the children on how what you have done will make other people happy. Children can pretend to be good little elves (invisible, of course) who clean up the house or do other good turns. Mother will "wonder" who could have done it.

E. *Sharing games.*

*1. Feeding each other: at lunchtime, tie splints to children's arms so they can't bend their elbows. Ask, "How are you going to eat?" (They will have to feed each other.)

*2. Sharing tools: Pass out molding clay but give each child only one tool (one a roller, one a cookie cutter, etc.). Ask, "How can you make everything you want with only one tool?" (They can share tools.)

III. Family Focal Point: The Family Round Table

We have a big round table in the family room. Whenever a family member finds something worth sharing—a special picture, a pretty rock, a new book, anything he wants to pass around—it is put on the round table. Children, aware of that table and the opportunity they have to put something on it, seem to become more oriented not only to sharing but also to observing, to finding something worthwhile to share. It needn't be a round table; it could be any place that's out of the reach of infants and pets, a place designated for the joy of sharing.

IV. Story: "The Sharing Tree"

"Please don't make me push them any further," little Oakley pleaded. "It's so cold and damp down there, and I keep bumping into rocks." The baby oak tree was about to cry when Oakhurst, the grand old oak standing beside him, explained again, "Now Oakley, my son, soon it will be spring, with hard spring winds, and then summer, with summer storms. Your roots must be strong to hold the rest of you in place. They must be deep in the rich, moist soil to find nourishing food to make your trunk and branches sturdy and healthy. By next year you will have grown so much, you won't believe it!" "Very well," sighed Oakley with a sad but determined grunt. He pushed his roots deeper into the ground, a little further each day, until spring arrived.

One warm, beautiful spring day, Oakley glanced over at his branches and was amazed to see beautiful green buds all over his tips. He thought they were gorgeous, and he was feeling great until one day he started to feel that his beautiful buds were about to burst. "Oh, Oakhurst," he gasped as he looked at his magnificent friend beside him, "my branches, my beautiful branches! They're about to burst and I can't stop them, no matter how hard I try!" "My dear Oakley," smiled the big, calm tree, "stop trying! Instead of losing something, you'll find a pleasant surprise. You must learn that when you let go of something very precious to you, it will be replaced by something better." Because he trusted his kind friend so much, Oakley reluctantly let go. Almost like hundreds of little jack-in-the-boxes, tiny green leaves began to appear all over his branches. "Oh, look at me now! " Oakley cried. "You were right! "

As days passed, Oakley became more and more beautiful. He loved the feeling of the wind rustling through his leaves, but the thing that made him happiest was to watch the lovely family of robins who had built their home in his branches. They were happy there, and that made Oakley happy too. He was so glad that he was strong and sturdy with deep roots and that he was sharing with others the beauty and comfort of his leaves. Before long he noticed little brown seeds beginning to form, which Oakhurst told him were acorns; he was proud of them too.

One day as he was watching the robin children play, he noticed that his leaves were not so green. Some had even begun to turn gold, and one of his acorns fell off, and then another, and then another and another. "Stop! " he screamed. "I need you all to keep me beautiful! " But they continued to fall, and he shouted, "Oakhurst, what is happening? I'm changing color, and my acorns are falling! " "Don't be afraid," said Oakhurst kindly. "Remember what I said to you before. Any time you give up something very special to you, you are giving service and it will always be replaced by something better. Soon you will lose all your acorns. Many of them will be gathered up by our little friends the squirrels, who will store them for food for the winter so they won't be hungry when all the berries have gone. Some will even find a warm spot in the earth, and then when spring comes, they will sprout roots of their own and begin to grow. And you'll find that you'll turn from green to gorgeous orange and red, and then the weather will turn cold and you'll lose all your leaves! " "Lose all my leaves! " shrieked Oakley. "Then I will be ugly and cold, and I'll never grow to be so wise and beautiful as *you.* " "Ah, you are wrong, my little friend," said the grand old Oakhurst. "That's exactly how I became wise and strong."

At the time, Oakley thought that was all very strange, but as the days passed he began to realize what his friend meant. He saw his acorns drop and his little friends gather them for winter food. His leaves turned a beautiful red, and then, just as Oakhurst had said, they began to drop off. He was sad at first, but when he saw the children rustling through them and having so much fun playing in them, he was glad for the opportunity to share. And when the cold winter came (and Oakley did look a bit ugly some days) he was happy that he had shared himself. He knew that when springtime came again he would be stronger, his roots would be longer, his leaves and branches would be bigger, and he would be better . . . and more like his great friend Oakhurst.

V. Reading List

Bonsall, C. *It's Mine, the Greedy Book.* New York: Harper & Row Publishers, 1964.

Brown, M. *Benjy's Blanket.* New York: Franklin Watts, 1962.

_____. *Company's Coming for Dinner.* New York: Franklin Watts, 1959.

Flack, M. *Ask Mr. Bear.* New York: The Macmillan Co., 1932.

Monsell, H. A. *Paddy's Christmas.* New York: Alfred A. Knopf, 1942.

Odor, R. *Lori's Day.* Chicago: Child's World, 1977.

_____. *Sarah Lou's Untied Shoe.* Chicago: Child's World, 1976.

Riley, S. *What Does It Mean? Help!* Chicago: Children's Press, 1978.

_____. *What Does It Mean? Sharing.* Chicago: Children's Press, 1978.

Silverstein, S. *The Giving Tree.* New York: Harper & Row Publishers, 1964.

Zolotow, C. *Do You Know What I'll Do?* New York: Harper & Row Publishers, 1958.

_____. *Mr. Rabbit and the Lovely Present.* New York: Harper & Row Publishers, 1962.

VI. Postscript

A. One day Ryan, age four, said, "Teacher, I really fooled my mom last night." His eyes sparkled with joy as he continued, "While she was in the bedroom with the baby, I set the table. I was *very* quiet. When she came in the kitchen to finish dinner she was so surprised. She just couldn't figure out who did it, and I didn't tell."

B. After our unit on sharing and service, many of the children at the Joy School (especially the older ones) seem to really enjoy helping others to zip their coats, put on boots, find where a puzzle piece goes, or put away the blocks. At clean-up time, everyone joins in and helps each other with very little help or suggestion from the teacher.

Index

Academic skill, early, 88-90

Achieving, games and stories that teach joy of, 112, 117

Activity board, 64

Answer and ask, 85-86

Answer prayer out loud, 41

Ant colony, 74

"Aren't we blessed" game, 40

Attempts, praise of, 127-28

Awareness of each other, 138

Backyard, Josh discovers the, 72-73

Badges, "I'm special," 153

"Bears Save the Baby, The," story, 51-54

Beauty in the earth, 70-71

Beggar, taken to lunch, 49

"Ben the Rich Boy," story, 64-66

Blind man, making friends with, 180-81

Bodily skills, developing, 62-63

Body: teaching joy of, 58-67; teaching appreciation of, 60-61

Body parts, learning names of, 60

Books, on raising children, 3; about each child, 152-53; "empty," 154-55

Boston, observant tourist sees, 84-85

Cabin, building with family, 109

Calmness of home, protecting, 20-21

Candor, honesty, realness, 160-69

Care of the body, 63

Caution, overdone, 123

Checklist, things able to do before attending school, 89-90

"Cheekey and the Laws," story, 33-34

"Chest," private, 155

Childlike faith, 18-19, 38-39

Christmas: traditions, 140-42; card list, 172

Club, exclusive, for each child, 153-54

Colors, to know before attending school, 90

Communication, 170-77

Comparisons, make children feel inferior, 123

Confidence, losing joy of, 122-23

Consistency, 138

Consultants, mothers as, 87

Creativity, 101-2

Curiosity and interest, 82-93

Daddy dates, 128, 154

Decisions, right and wrong, 26-27

Devotionals, family, 21-22

Dickens, Charles, 38

Differences, 152

Disagreement, parental, 164

Discipline, 30-31

Dog, baby laughing at, 48

Ear infection, blessing child ill with, 18

Early academic skill, 88-90

Early-morning "quiet time," 21
"Earth Ernie," story, 76-78
Earth, teaching joy of, 68-80
Emotional joys, 7
Encouragement: liberal, 99; lack of, in preserving trust, 122-23; understand need for, 127
"Epamanatus," story, 103-4
Example: of children, learn from, 85; lack of, in experiencing new things, 122
Exclusive club for each child, 153-54
Experts board, 155-56
Explore and compare, 20

Failures and mistakes, 113-14
Fairy tales, 50
Faith: childlike, 18-19, 38-39; preserving joy of, 16-23
Family: devotionals, 21-22; prayer, 22; security, identity, pride in, 132-45; strong, as neighbors, 134-35; "institution," 137
Family focal points, 8-9; laws chart, 31-32; testimony meeting, 41-42; treasure chest, 51; activity board, ·64; "records list," 64; favorite things wall, 75-76; interest book, 90-91; Mommy-Daddy proud board, 102-3; Sunday goal-setting sessions, 114-15; Daddy and Mommy dates, 128; traditions, 139-42; experts board, 155-56; happys and sads, 166; "guess who's coming to dinner," 176; round table, 185-86
Farmer who loves senses, 58-59
Fasting, 40-41
Fatherhood, 1-2
"Favorite things wall," 40, 75-76
Feelings, acceptability of showing, 165
"Fluffy Needs His Family," story, 142-43

Focal points. See Family focal points
Forgetting self, 182-84
Four-season collections, 74
Franklin, Benjamin, 136

Games: group, 50; sharing, 185
Genealogy, 137-38
Gifts, help children discover own, 152
Goal setting, 108-12, 114-15
Good deeds, 185
Gratitude, synonymous with joy, 15; teaching joy of, 38-44; display, for children, 138-39
"Growing bottle," 74
"Guess who's coming to dinner," 176
"Gunny bag," 113

Happys and sads, 166
Harvard study of "A" mothers and "C" mothers, 86-88
Harvest, law of, 112-13
Hawaiian beach party, 123-24
Help less fortunate, 184
"Herman Finds a Friend," story, 176
"Hoky Poky," game, 60
Holy Ghost, gift of, 18-19
Home, keeping Spirit in, 20; protect calmness of, 20-21; bringing spiritual influences into, 21-22
Honesty, realness, candor, 160-69
"How Heavenly Father Helped Me," story, 22

Ideal place to raise children, 137
Identity, pride, family security, 132-45
Imagination, 98-99, 102
Independence at early age, 151-52
Individual, know each child as, 151
Inherent joys, preserving, 8
Inhibitions, 60, 97-98
Initiative of child, 86-88
"Interest": games, 88; stories, 88; book, 90-91

"I.Q." vs. "J.Q.," 13
"Isabel's Little Lie," story, 166-67

"Jason and the Circus Money," story, 115-17
Joy: one gift to give children, 4-5; synonymous with gratitude, 15
Joys: children born with, 6-7; deciding which to teach, 7; learned, 8; identifying, 8
"Joy School," 5-6, 12

Kennedy, Rose, 125-26
Knowing God as Father, 38-40

Law of harvest, 112-13
Laws, necessary for happiness, 28
Learning lines for Sunday School part, 109-10
Letters, child to know before attending school, 90
Love, unconditional, 150

"Maisey and Daisey," story, 91-92
Making things, 99-100
Managers, mothers as, 87-88
McKay, David O., 26
Mistakes: in answering child's questions, 86; and failure, 113-14
Mommy-Daddy proud board, 102-3
Mr. Nobody visits Joy School, 105

Nature, 73-74
Nicknames, 154
Nursery schools, 4

Obedience, 27-28; "perfect," 29
Observant, children are, 84
"One Thing I Like About You," game, 152
Opening packages, 50
Opportunities for decision-making, 29-30
Order and organization, 113

Ozzie and Harriet, TV show, 20-21

Painting, stimulus to creativity, 96-97
Parental disagreement, 164
"Pedro the Squirrel," story, 128-29
"Perfect obedience," 29
"Ping Pong Ball and the Christmas Tree Bulb, The," story, 156-57
Politician, story of honest, 163-64
"Popcorn dance," 142
Praise, 127-28, 164-65
Pratt, Parley P., 18-19
Prayer: family, 22, 40; answer out loud, 41
Premortal existence, role play, 40
Preschools, 4
Pretending, 100
Pride, identity, family security, 132-45
Priorities, order, goals, 106-18
Problem solving, 100
Professor, confident, 148-49
Proud board, Mommy-Daddy, 102-3
Punishments, 31, 32
Puzzle: of body, 60; doing without eyes or hands, 61

"Records list," 64
Red bicycle vs. silver bicycle, 27-28
Regularity of family prayer, 22
Reinforcement and praise, 164-65
Relationships, 170-77
Relive spontaneous moments, 50
Respect each child, 151
Responsibility at early age, 151-52
"Rock Game," 152
Role-play: premortal existence, 40; relationship problems, 174-75

Seeing in the mind, 99
Self-reliance at early age, 151-52
Senses chart, 62, 73
Sensory stimulation, 61

Service: and sharing, 178-89; within
   family, 184-85
Shapes, to know before attending
   school, 90
Sharing and service, 178-89
"Sharing Tree, The," story, 186-88
Silly things, to teach spontaneity,
   50-51
"Simon Says," 60
Situations governed by law vs. de-
   cisions, 28-29
Skills, bodily, 62-63
Skipping, learning, 149-50
Snap-judging, 127
Solving problems, 100
Sounds, identify, 61
Spiritual influences, bringing into
   home, 21-22
Spontaneity, 48-55
Stewardship of father, 3
Stimulation, 88
Stradivari, Antonio, 149
Sunday goal-setting, 114-15
Surprise-oriented group games, 50

Terminology of earth, 73

Testimony meeting, family, 41-42
Thoughtfulness in family prayer, 22
Times to Remember by Rose Kennedy,
   125-26
Traditions, family, 139-42
Treasure chest, family, 51
Trust, 122-23, 126
Try new things, 127

Uniqueness, help child be secure in,
   153
Uses of nature, 74-75

"What is it?" game, 61
"Which is the best way?" game, 175
Wise and foolish decisions, stories of,
   30
Working together, 139

Young, Brigham: on parental ties,
   15; on children's faith, 18; on
   goals and order, 108; on teaching
   only true things, 122; on studying
   children, 148; on honesty, 162; on
   bickering, 172
"Your Story," 42-43